THE ANSWER
IS THE SPIRIT

by
R. E. O. WHITE

THE WESTMINSTER PRESS
Philadelphia

Published by The Westminster Press ®
Philadelphia, Pennsylvania

PRINTED IN THE UNITED STATES OF AMERICA

9 8 7 6 5 4 3 2 1

Library of Congress Cataloging in Publication Data

White, Reginald E   O
  The answer is the spirit.

  Bibliography: p.
  Includes index.
  1. Holy Spirit—Biblical teaching. I. Title.
BS680.H56W45   231'.3   79-23825
ISBN 0-664-24311-8

Contents

CHAPTER ONE

'Let's be practical'

Five short narratives, a few letters, a handful of tracts and an underground pamphlet—nothing could look less like a textbook on religion than our New Testament. It is hardly a treatise on doctrine, certainly not a blueprint for heaven; it most resembles a driver's handbook designed to keep the working Christian on the road. We might call it a do-it-yourself manual for pilgrims, if it did not constantly warn that you cannot do-it-yourself. Above all, the New Testament is, and was always meant to be, a 'How to . . .' book, a guide to actually living the Christian life.

An exception might be made for *Acts*, essentially a defence of Christianity, represented by Paul, before people in authority in the Roman empire, like 'his Excellency, Theophilus'. And perhaps for *Romans*, which is manifestly an appeal for support for a proposed mission to Spain though, to meet possible objections, the letter includes a full explanation of Paul's position on several disputed points. For the rest the epistles are pastoral counsel offered at a distance, substituting for a visit or preparatory to one, and offering guidance on innumerable practical questions. The gospels were produced in the greater churches to recall and record what was said and done by Jesus, as his words and deeds threw light on various problems thrown up in church life—paying taxes, exorcisms, the sabbath, marriage questions, and a host of others. *Revelation* was written to encourage seven named Asian churches, and stiffen their resistance before a coming wave of persecution.

Of course, such pastoral instruction and advice provides a unique quarry from which to dig materials to construct Christian theology. Theology is there, a necessary part of the instruction, and basis of the advice. Frequently we can see the doctrine actually in process of being hammered out in response to some problem or heresy troubling a Christian group. The doctrine of Christ so forcefully presented in *Philippians* 2 is evoked by the need for a similar selfless, self-emptying spirit among certain Philippian Christians; a similar passage in *Colossians* 1 is Paul's energetic answer to inadequate ideas of Christ affecting the Colossians' worship and behaviour. The intense theological meditation of *1 John* is in reply to wrong notions about Christ's incarnation which had led to schism among the churches John knew, and to a dangerous moral permissiveness.

We mishandle the New Testament, and get the teaching tangled and out of focus, whenever we forget that the theology is 'being done' (as the current phrase has it) in the midst of a busy church beset with manifold questions and problems. Paul and the rest had little interest, if any at all, in systematic doctrine or religious speculation. Doctrine was thought through, and applied, with practical, pastoral intent: to assess it correctly, we must always consider it in the light of actual situations it was designed to meet, the daily experience of ordinary Christian people which it was intended to express, and to enrich. To forget this, is

2

like trying to understand the theory of swimming without ever getting wet.

It would be exaggeration to contend that this is the only way to explore the great promise of the Spirit to the Christian believer. But it is no exaggeration to say it is the way that the New Testament expounds the subject. The doctrine of the Spirit was, and is, an essential truth of the Christian faith, but it found expression and elaboration in the New Testament documents as a prescription against certain ills, a provision for all-round spiritual health, an answer to meet specific, definable needs and situations. To study in this way what the New Testament says about the Spirit, *and why*, has great advantages. It delivers from that laborious collection of isolated texts and half-texts and phrases to make up our own 'systematic doctrine', in which theologians delight; and it enables us instead to listen to what the New Testament actually sets out to say. What is even more important, we are able, to some degree, to watch the first Christians thinking out their faith in the Spirit as life itself taught them, step by step, their need of his gifts and instruction, his presence and power.

That God should thus endue his servants with special gifts, capacities, insights and power matched to their needs, opportunities and responsibilities, is of course an element in all religious faith. Jews with the Old Testament in their hands, or in their hearts, would think it self-evident that God bestows all that is needful for his work. Curiously, like the word 'talent' from the parable, the term 'gift' has in common speech come to mean a *natural* endowment or capacity, for music, eloquence, art, diplomacy and the like. In biblical use it means always the opposite, something not native to man but bestowed by God for special purpose and responsibility.

The New Testament term *charisma* has suffered an even worse fate: it was once defined, in a televised interview, as 'sex appeal plus the gift of the gab': that is denigration beyond measure! The root word, *charis* means simply *favour*, the free, totally undeserved, but overflowing and variegated (*1 Peter* 4:10) favour which God shows towards his people, and by which he gives to us freely, without thought of merit, what-ever pertains to life and to salvation. From the Latin word for such free favour shown by one in power towards a suppliant, come the corresponding words 'grace' and 'gratis'—a gift or favour given free. *Anything* freely bestowed by the favour of God is a *charisma*, and the list of such gifts in the New Testament is almost endless.

The whole Christian salvation is a *charisma* of God (*Romans* 5:15), and so is eternal life (*Romans* 6:23). So are all divine privileges (*Romans* 11:29), encourage-ment (*Romans* 1:11), continence in sex (*1 Corinthians* 7:7), deliverance from peril (*2 Corinthians* 1:11), teaching and pastoral ability (*1 Timothy* 4:14), speak-ing and serving (*1 Peter* 4:10, 11), exhortation, generosity, assistance to others, almsgiving (*Romans* 12:6f), wisdom, knowledge, faith, healing, other miracles, prophecy, distinguishing between spirits, speaking in 'tongues', interpretation of 'tongues' (*1 Corinthians* 12:4f). And there is no reason to think the grace-gifts mentioned exhaust the ways in which the measureless grace of God may be shown towards us. It is well to repeat, in New Testament language *every expression of the divine favour is a charisma*; two or more are *charismata*; and everyone who experiences such divine favour, in any form, is a *charismatic*.

Some of these gifts of grace, however, are especially associated with the presence and power of the Holy Spirit in the Christian's life, or in the church—namely the nine above listed from *1 Corinthians* 12, which are expressly described as *charismata* given by the Spirit. It is dangerous to forget that these too are gifts of divine grace and favour, no more to be merited, claimed, deserved, or earned, than is salvation, or eternal life. To discuss 'how to obtain' such gifts, as a kind of bonus paid out to Christians whose faith works overtime; or 'how to lay claim' to the gifts of the Spirit—as if any *gift* could ever be *claimed*; to seek them for enjoyment, for display, to confirm faith, or to increase our own spiritual self-esteem by a strange 'charismatic self-righteousness', is to miss entirely the simple meaning of the gospel word *charisma*—'gift of God's favour'. The Spirit 'apportions to each one individually as he wills', and the purpose is always 'for the common good' (*1 Corinthians* 12:11, 7). To God the Spirit alone it belongs to give or to withhold: ours only to receive with gratitude, and use with humility for the practical purposes for which the gifts are bestowed.

If it be asked why some of these favours should be ascribed especially to *the Spirit* of God, the answer is not far to seek. Israel's faith had for centuries been nourished on the thought of the God who is everywhere, and everywhere powerful. Whatever moved or changed without visible cause, there 'spirit' was at work: the drifting sand, the driving clouds, the bending trees and tossing waves all offered evidence of invisible moving forces that wrought wonderful—and sometimes terrible—effects. The wind, or breath, of

God was thus a natural and vivid metaphor for his invisible but powerful presence in his world. Indeed, was not man himself, at first, but a sculptured model of clay under the fingers of God, until God 'breathed into his nostrils the breath of life, and man became a living being' (*Genesis* 2:7)?

Forbidden to make any visible representation of God, the Jew could think of him only as pure, 'disembodied' Spirit—if he thought in that abstract way at all. In fact, the Jew learned through everyday experience, in intensely practical ways: only afterwards did he reflect on the truth implied. In the Old Testament as in the New, the Spirit was the answer, and the explanation, to needs, emergencies, and problems that had to be faced. When need arose, at the erection of the Tabernacle, for men of 'ability and intelligence, with knowledge and all craftsmanship, to devise artistic designs, to work in gold, silver, and bronze, in cutting stones for setting, and in carving wood, for work in every craft', and for embroiderers and weavers, with ability to impart to others their taste and skill, it was to the 'inspiration' of men 'filled with the Spirit of God' that Israel turned (*Exodus* 31: 1–5; 35: 30–35).

When need arose for a successor to Moses, they sought 'a man in whom is the Spirit' (*Numbers* 27:18), and when enemies oppressed beyond endurance, 'the Spirit of the Lord began to stir' a mighty guerrilla leader named Samson to prodigious deeds (*Judges* 13: 25; 14: 6, 19; 15:14). Later the Spirit moved young Saul to prophesy in God's name (*1 Samuel* 10:10–12)—as a sign that the hand of God was upon him for some special task. Such gifts appear to have been conferred on unexpected individuals, for a brief time and for some limited purpose, sometimes with odd results; later, the Spirit is seen to come upon men chosen for a life-work, as the Spirit of wisdom, of truth, of prophecy, the source of revelation, the giver of visions, the interpreter of events, and even of dreams, the one through whom the word of God comes to God's spokesmen in bewildering and tragic days (*Numbers* 24:2; 11:26; *Jeremiah* 23:21–22, and often).

With the catastrophe of the Exile, far-reaching insights are gained into the way in which the Spirit equips for emergencies. As the future darkened, Jeremiah looked to a new covenant between the people and God, based on forgiveness and a change of heart, as the only hope for his nation. How it was to be achieved, Jeremiah does not say: he seems to have expected that the years of suffering would teach their own deep lesson. Ezekiel lived to see that suffering could harden obstinacy, and embitter despairing hearts, and so he looked to a more radical solution—when God would cleanse the nation once again, giving a new heart and new spirit by putting his Spirit within them: then the people would rise from their desolation and decay like a great army *resurrected* to new life by the breath of God, who promises 'I will put my Spirit within you, and you shall live' (*Ezekiel* 36:25f; 37: 1–14).

Joel's great promise of the out-pouring of the Spirit echoes Ezekiel's perceptive confidence. When the exiles returned in weakness to a land in ruin, Haggai pleaded for the re-establishment of the Temple as the key to the future; Zechariah pinned his hope to human leadership of prince and priest; but Joel realised clearly that only a spiritual renewal of the whole people could ensure that Judah fulfilled the purposes of God:

> And it shall come to pass afterward
>   that I will pour out my Spirit on all flesh;
> your sons and your daughters shall prophesy,
>   your old men shall dream dreams,
>   and your young men shall see visions.
> Even upon the menservants and maidservants
>   in those days, I will pour out my Spirit . . .

Not by rebuilding the institutions only, nor by aristocratic leadership, but in the regeneration of the common people, lay the ultimate promise that

> My people shall never again be put to shame . . .
> (Joel 2:26–29)

This growing understanding of the practical importance of the Spirit to the intentions of God for Israel, as the Spirit of exceptional powers, of insight into truth, and of renewed life, is brought to focus in the promise of Messiah. For he is to be equipped for his task by the Spirit of wisdom and understanding, of counsel and might, of knowledge and the fear of the Lord—all the equipment required to *rule*; while the same Spirit shall anoint him to bring good tidings to the afflicted, to bind up the brokenhearted, proclaim liberty to the captives, the opening of the prison to them that are bound—all the equipment required to *save* (*Isaiah* 11:1–3; 61:1–4). The glory to come is thus seen to depend upon a Spirit-endowed Messiah amid a Spirit-indwelt people: already the whole thought of the Spirit of God is moving towards identification with the Christ who is to come.

In the years between the Testaments, one other shift of thought lent definition and urgency to the expectation that the age of Messiah would see the triumph of God's Spirit. For, probably under foreign influence, an elaborate demonology came to be widely accepted among the Jews, which held that the world was infested with two or three million demon-spirits, invisible, ubiquitous, malign, the source of illness, madness, and all that was degrading and corrupt. Before these 'principalities and powers', 'spirits of the height and of the depth', 'spirits at work in the disobedient', man was wholly vulnerable; when once they were allowed to take 'possession', he was helpless—unless the Spirit of God should intervene. We shall not *feel* what the early Christians *felt* about the promise of the Spirit to indwell believers, until we understand the panic fears, the dread helplessness, which belief in evil spirits can create. The very name by which we know the Spirit of Christ is due to this direct contrast—vital to the early Christians' sense of liberation and joy—between the evil spirits that everywhere threatened their lives, and the one *Holy* Spirit who brought them freedom, purity, sanity and power.

Thus by long training in the ways of God, and hard experience of the vicissitudes of life, Jewish minds were well prepared to look to the living, moving, powerful, illuminating, sanctifying Spirit of God for the abilities, courage, and qualities of character which life demanded of them. From first to last, their understanding of God's Spirit was no speculation about the nature of the Godhead, but the practical answer to some felt necessity, the resolution of some recurrent problem, the way out of some spiritual crisis. This was the Old Testament's promise, as it was the early church's experience, that in every practical emergency: the answer is the Spirit.

CHAPTER TWO

Allusions and assumptions

If our contention is correct, that the experience of the Holy Spirit is in the New Testament related directly, and always, to practical problems and needs, then we would expect to find that those New Testament books which have no particular problem in view would speak less of the Spirit than those addressed to specific difficulties—the fewer the problems, the less talk of the Spirit. On a review of every clear reference to the Spirit in the New Testament (see the index to this present study, p. 159), this is precisely what we find.

Teaching about the Spirit is distributed very unequally through the New Testament's pages. Some books scarcely refer to the subject at all, and often what is said is merely *reminiscent*, recalling past experiences of the Spirit, or the voice of the Spirit in scripture, rather than exhorting or instructing with a view to new experience. Moreover, what is said in some passages is plainly allusive and *incidental*, not the main subject under discussion, the theme of any particular argument, or the object of writing. Then, too, the references to the Spirit are sometimes *ambiguous*: printers of the Bible, even of the Greek text, or the committees who instruct them, vary greatly in their use of a capital letter for the word, and occasionally it is far from clear whether the Spirit of God, the human spirit, or a mere human disposition or attitude, is meant. For example, the *Revised Standard Version* of *Acts* 6:10 says that the Jews could not withstand the wisdom and the Spirit with which Stephen spoke; the *Authorised Version* mentions simply Stephen's 'wisdom and spirit'; the *New English Bible* says it was his 'inspired wisdom' which confounded them. In *Romans* 8:15, *RSV* says 'you did not receive the spirit of slavery . . . but . . . the spirit of sonship'; *AV* gives the second 'spirit' a capital, though not the first.

We must not look, therefore, for mention of the Holy Spirit everywhere in the New Testament, nor expect it everywhere to be given equal importance. On the other hand, we must be careful what conclusions we draw from the facts we find. Sometimes an experience may be referred to infrequently because it is rare, and little understood; sometimes because it is so commonplace as to be taken entirely for granted.

Paul's letter to the Colossians does deal with a serious theological question which had arisen within that church, yet it mentions the Holy Spirit only once, and then almost incidentally: 'Epaphras . . . has made known to us your love in the Spirit' (1:8). The relation of the Spirit to Christian love, here merely assumed, is made a central theme elsewhere. In his letters to the Thessalonians, Paul refers to the Spirit twice when recalling the power and joy with which they first received the gospel (*1 Thessalonians* 1:5, 6), and (probably) twice in connection with sanctification. Warning against sexual uncleanness, Paul adds significantly, 'Whoever disregards this, disregards not man but God, who gives his Holy Spirit to you' (*1 Thessalonians* 4:8, echoed apparently in *2 Thessalonians* 2:13): this connection also, of the Spirit with sexual sanctification, is fully treated elsewhere, here simply taken for granted. The remaining terse reference, 'Quench not the Spirit' (5:19), since it is followed by 'do not despise prophesying', seems to refer to the free responsiveness of the assembled believers to the movement of the Spirit in Christian worship, though no such explanation is offered. It seems fair to assume that original teaching about the Spirit as convicting of the truth, conferring joy, sanctifying the believer's body and inspiring the church's worship, is all being presupposed: there is no further instruction, because the situation at Thessalonica did not call for it.

The note of news, explanation, warning and thanks which Paul sent to Philippi speaks of his hopes of deliverance 'through your prayers and the help of the Spirit of Jesus Christ' (1:19)—Paul seems to expect the Spirit to intervene in his imprisonment.'Participation [or, fellowship] in the Spirit' (2:1) and 'worship . . . in spirit' (3:3) are unfortunately less confident translations, but there is no question that both thoughts occur frequently in the New Testament, so that decision is unnecessary. No urgent problem required further exposition of the ministry of the Spirit.

The long and eloquent treatise we know as the *Epistle to the Hebrews* mentions the Spirit three times as the one who speaks through scripture (3:7; 9:8; 10:15). This thought was evidently too familiar to need comment; it follows naturally from the Old Testament idea of the Spirit as the source of prophecy. Three further allusions recall the early Christian experience of the readers, when 'God also bore witness by signs and wonders and various miracles and by gifts of the Holy Spirit distributed according to his own will'; those who have been once enlightened are assumed to have become partakers of the Holy Spirit; and those who turn back from Christ are described as 'outraging the Spirit of grace' (2:4; 6:4; 10:29).

These are vital insights into the place of the Spirit in Christian experience. That the Spirit brings conviction to the convert's heart, sometimes by miracles and signs; that all Christians participate in the Spirit—the phrase 'gifts of the Spirit' here means dispensings, or 'distributions' not of other things *by* the Spirit, but of the Spirit himself to believers, so that they become 'partakers' of the Spirit; that such 'dispensings' of the Spirit are entirely at his own will, and not at our command; and that to desert Christ is therefore to do outrage to the Spirit who in God's grace first brought us into the Christian way—these are the very foundations of New Testament teaching about the Spirit. Yet in this letter they are not so much taught as recalled, familiar truths already sufficiently known, and held in common by writer and readers—'elementary stuff'!

In one moving phrase, it would appear that the Spirit is in this epistle brought into closest relation with Christ in his atoning death: '. . . how much more shall the blood of Christ, who through [the] eternal Spirit offered himself without blemish to God, purify your conscience . . .' (9:14). It is not as clear as we would wish whether this means 'through the Holy Spirit'. The point the writer is making (among others) is that, in contrast with the old covenant and sanctuary and sacrifices, which were temporary, Christ's priesthood and death provide 'eternal redemption . . . an eternal offering . . . an eternal inheritance' (9:12, 14, 15). As Jesus holds his priesthood, not by temporary legal enactment but 'by the power of an indestructible life' (7:16), so his sacrifice, though offered once in time, at the end of the age, yet has eternal efficacy and power, unlike the sacrifices of old (9:26, 14). His is 'a spiritual and eternal sacrifice' (*NEB*). If more than this is meant, it is probably because as Servant of the Lord, Christ was anointed by the Spirit for his work (*Isaiah* 42:1), and so as in his ministry, so in his atonement, all he does is in virtue of the Spirit's endowment—though that is easier to say than to explain.

Since *Hebrews* deals throughout with the temptation to recede from Christian commitment in face of threatening persecution, it is surprising that positive, direct teaching about the Spirit who might strengthen faith and stiffen courage is not given. It is useless to speculate why, except to notice that not every strand of New Testament thought would turn automatically to this theme for the relevant word.

The newly baptised who (it is generally thought) are addressed in *1 Peter* are reminded that it was by the Spirit they were set apart, or 'sanctified' for God; and that those who brought them the gospel were also empowered by the Spirit sent from heaven—the same Spirit of truth who in the ancient prophets had foretold the suffering and the glory of Christ (1:2, 11, 12). Once more the place of the Spirit in the initiation of Christian experience is assumed as familiar between writer and readers: if it is true that these opening chapters were once a baptismal address, the point has added significance. The only other reference to the Spirit (3:18; 4:6 hardly count here) is 4:14: 'If you are reproached for the name of Christ, you are blessed, because the Spirit of glory and of God rests upon you.' So translated, the words recall the blessing Jesus pronounced upon those who suffer for righteousness' sake (and possibly also the descent of the Spirit to 'rest upon' him at his baptism): a reminder which must have brought true comfort and strength to young Christian hearts facing their first persecution, especially if they knew the promise of Jesus, 'When they deliver you up, do not be anxious how you are to speak or what you are to say: for what you are to say will be given you in that hour; for it is not you who speak, but the Spirit of your Father speaking through you' (*Matthew* 10:19, 20).

2 Peter's only mention of the Spirit echoes once more the thought that the Spirit moved the men of God of old to write the prophetic scripture (1:21). For *Jude*, it is the ultimate charge to be laid against heretics, schismatics, the worldly, that they 'have not the Spirit'; in contrast with those diligent to build themselves up upon their faith, and keep themselves in the love of God, by praying 'in the Holy Spirit' (19, 20). *James*' only use of the word is in 4:5, 'the scripture says, He yearns jealously over the spirit which he has made to dwell in us', which almost certainly means the human spirit. In that case, *James* like *Philemon*, and *2 John*, *3 John*, does not mention the Holy Spirit.

The so-called Pastoral Epistles sent to Timothy and Titus are often said to be more pedestrian in tone than earlier New Testament writing. Gone, we are told, is the abounding joy, the excited expectation of the Advent, the confidence in Christian salvation so victorious and vigorous that mean temptations (like pilfering and drunkenness in 'bishops'!) present no perils; gone too are the miraculous gifts bestowed by the Spirit on ordinary men and women to equip them for Christian office. Instead, a careful examination is to be made of those available, and lists are drawn up of the qualities required in suitable applicants! It is necessary now to 'give attention' to adding good behaviour to sound doctrine, to 'exercise oneself' in godliness. It all has a nostalgic air, recommending a cautious, down-to-earth organisation of Christian life for testing days stretching ahead. So far as this description is true, it brings the Pastoral Epistles closer to our own actual experience of the Christian faith than, say, the *Book of Acts* or *1 Corinthians* are: and what the Pastorals have to say about the Spirit is consequently more relevant to ourselves.

But it is not much. The quoted stanza of an early hymn in *1 Timothy* 3:16 speaks of the Spirit as 'vindicating' Christ: his presence and power at Pentecost and in the subsequent life of the church is repeatedly cited as 'confirming' the gospel message concerning Christ, with signs and wonders, demonstrations of the Spirit and of power. The following verse, 4:1, adds a further reference to the continuing ministry of the Spirit in the church: 'the Spirit expressly says that in later times some will depart from the faith . . .' evidently cites what Christian prophets are known to have been saying in the worship services of the church. From the details of the warning that are given, it is less likely to be a reference to the Spirit speaking through the scriptures. In *2 Timothy* 1:7 the 'spirit of timidity' describes a mood or disposition of soul; 'a spirit of power, love, and self-control' may likewise mean a disposition of the Christian—or, possibly, the Spirit who creates it, since power, love, and sanctification are regularly ascribed to the Spirit elsewhere. In *2 Timothy* 1:14 the young pastor is urged to guard the truth entrusted to him by the Holy Spirit, probably at his setting apart for Christian service

(*1 Timothy* 4:14). He is also reminded (as ministers sometimes need to be reminded) that the indwelling of the Spirit is the privilege of *all* believers.

If these slight allusions do not add much to our knowledge of the Spirit, it is important to note that they are still being made in a period when 'the spiritual temperature has dropped'. Christian conviction, the Christian's mood, and Christian service are, even in such a time, still understood to depend upon the Spirit. And so does Christian conversion. In *Titus* 3:5 the beginning of Christian life is wonderfully described as 'the washing of regeneration and renewal in the Holy Spirit, which he poured on us richly through Christ our Saviour . . .' The reception of the Spirit at conversion (associated, probably, with the 'washing' of baptism), the total renewal of life in Christ, the enduement with the Spirit, if not 'without measure' (as was written of Jesus), at any rate 'richly' for fullness of Christian living, are all themes familiar in earlier pages of the New Testament, and here reaffirmed with un-diminished clarity—even though the slightly formal expression may suggest the recital of a creed rather than the memory of an experience.

A Christian congregation may boast its carefully framed statement of convictions and principles that underlie its membership, but it is from the well-thumbed pages of its hymnbooks that the true tone and mood and emphases of their fellowship can be caught. Even so, reviewing these allusions, assumptions and reminiscences about the Spirit, thinly scattered over numerous pages of the New Testament, one discerns how sure these early Christians were that it was the Spirit who confirmed the gospel to them in signs and power and joy; who originally spoke through the scriptural prophecies and now made them come alive in the mouths of Christian evangelists; that it was the Spirit who purified their minds and hearts, and taught them love; that it was the Spirit, somehow closely related to Jesus, who had ushered them into a Spirit-filled community, in whose worship-sessions the Spirit himself moved and spoke with power. One feels with what certainty they knew the Spirit's indwelling, and that they, individually, were 'partakers' in the 'dispensing' of the Spirit. We sense also how sure they were that the Spirit was with them as they faced their persecutors, and would deliver them from suffering and from death as he saw fit.

None of these things is said, explicitly and plainly; they are taken for granted—which is perhaps the most significant feature to note. It is difficult to assess fairly the impression left by the infrequency of these references—some twenty-two or so in about one-sixth of the New Testament, or one reference in every fifty-five verses. Obviously, this should correct any over-emphasis which would treat an experience of the Spirit as the beginning and end of Christianity: teaching on the Spirit was not a central purpose of any of these letters, nor did these writers feel bound to draw attention to the topic. On the other hand, what is said implies that a fairly thorough explanation must already have been given when first the gospel reached these readers. Apostolic evangelism must have included considerable education on this as on other matters; as apostolic conversion clearly included an experience, a 'partaking' of the Spirit for every convert.

Yet it is not to these books we look for extended instruction on the Spirit in Christian experience, even as it is not to these we look for advice on any major spiritual or practical problem, for their counsel is, in the main, generalised and universal. That is no coincidence: it confirms our suggestion—the fewer the problems, the less talk of the Spirit. But where central and fundamental issues are under discussion, the answer is the Spirit.

CHAPTER THREE

The immense task

The Christian movement began with a world-pro-
gramme: by our time, the sheer audacity of it fails to
impress. Less than a dozen had wholly committed
themselves to Christ's cause, and humanly assessed
they were unpromising material for world-wide
venturing—fishermen, tax-collectors and the like, lay-
people with not a scribe or priest or rabbi among them.
Even spiritually they are unimpressive, for bewilderment, doubt, denial, fear, even ambition, had been
more in evidence in recent days than understanding,
or readiness for the future. It is impossible to miss the
absence of Peter, then Thomas, from the upper room
when the risen Christ appeared, and the omission of
five from the lakeside in Galilee—whatever we make
of it, the announcement by some, after all they had
seen and heard, that they 'go fishing' still strikes the
reader as odd. The emphasis laid by Jesus in the upper
room discourse upon loyalty to one another before the
world makes us wonder; and Luke's stress upon the
Spirit's coming when the disciples were all with one
accord in one place, almost implies that this was a
change!

Around this half-ready nucleus was a larger circle,
attached in varying degree to Christ, one hundred and
twenty, and a little later (as Paul records) 'above five

hundred brethren'. Five hundred to transform the world!

Doubtless some in that wider circle were from different levels of society, possessing varied expertise. The casting of lots to fill Judas' place is not afterwards appealed to for precedent, nor the method recommended to the churches, though it is saying too much to call it an act of desperation. Of individuals in the larger circle, little is heard later, except of James, a very new disciple, and a few of the women. Matched against the intention of a world-mission, in which nothing less than the continuation of the ministry of Jesus was planned (*Acts* 1:1–2), with all the problems of travel, language, acceptance in alien lands, transplanting the Palestine message into Gentile terms within a pagan culture, against intense religious and political opposition, the original disciple-band as *Acts* opens was not such as to frighten Caesar, or strike terror at the heart of the Empire.

The circumstances were equally unpropitious. In Jewry the scriptures were known, the prophecies revered, messianic expectation ran high in varied forms. In three years of ministry Jesus had manifested authority, winsomeness, compassion, and power beyond measure: he had come to his own, yet his own received him not. What prospect, then, of carrying the same message beyond Jewry into Caesar's world, where the whole climate of thought, morality, and expectation was different, and Jesus no more than a distant rumour out of the east? The mere recital of obvious immediate needs is intimidating: unity, leadership, power of communication, boldness, organisation, wisdom to face new situations, strategy to plan and accept new opportunities, a self-perpetuating drive for outreach, and a sense of authority and power that could attract, convince, and convert—and then hold. *Luke has no doubt that the single answer to all such practical problems surrounding the church's immense task was—the Holy Spirit.*

The way that, in *Acts*, the coming of the Spirit is promised indicates as much. It was in answer to a question about the future, about the restoration 'at this time' of the kingdom to Israel, that the risen Christ, speaking 'through the Holy Spirit' (1:2) repeated both the promise and the commission: 'It is not for you to know times or seasons which the Father has fixed by his own authority. But you shall receive power when the Holy Spirit has come upon you; and you shall be my witnesses in Jerusalem and in all Judea and Samaria and to the end of the earth.' And again is repeated the promise with which the whole Christian movement may be said to have been originally announced by John, as it is now inaugurated by Jesus: 'Wait for the promise . . . for John baptised with water, but before many days you shall be baptised with the Holy Spirit' (1:7, 8, 5).

In other words, curiosity about the future is not to be satisfied by forecasts: the future is to be explored, and made, in the power of the Spirit. Moreover, the Spirit is given here, not for the sake of the disciples, for their enjoyment and excitement, but for the sake of the outside world—for Jerusalem and Judea, for Samaria and the uttermost parts. The Spirit is not a reward for faith and loyalty, a thrilling experience to be sought and treasured for its own sake. In the very way that the promise is framed, the point is made unforgettably clear: the coming of the Spirit is the equipment for the task.

It is difficult to define precisely what happened when the promise was fulfilled at Pentecost. One thing abundantly clear is, that it was a miracle of communication. The word of God was spoken, with a Galilean accent (2:7), by uneducated, common men (4:13), and pilgrims to Jerusalem from various parts of the world heard and understood each in his own language (2:8). The speaker used his native language, and the listeners heard 'in tongues'—which were also varied 'native languages' (2:6–11).

Peter explained 'this that you see and hear' as a 'shedding forth' of the Spirit as promised by the Father and by the prophet Joel, enabling sons and daughters to prophesy, young men to see visions and old men to dream dreams—the qualifications of the prophet, the divine spokesman. Pentecost was essentially the fulfilment of the promise that the Spirit of prophecy should be universalised, as to age (old men, young men), class (you, your servants, your hand-maids), and sex (sons, daughters). The change that was manifest in Peter and the rest was likewise the mark of the prophet, the impulse to speak forth divine truth, the boldness to do so regardless of conse-quences, convicting the city of sin and rebellion against God, and calling for repentance. Peter is, in fact, suddenly a prophet. This, he says, is just what has happened: the implication is that the prophetic inspiration which after long silence had begun again in John was being continued in the disciples of Jesus—himself hailed as a prophet. The Spirit is expressly the Spirit of prophecy, speaking through David (1:16) and through Isaiah (28:25), resisted by Israel when continually speaking through the prophets (7:51), now manifest again in Christian prophets like Agabus

(11:27, 28) and the disciples newly baptised at Ephesus (19:6).

It was this prophetic boldness, their complete 'freedom of speech' as of men speaking under divine compulsion, in God's name and with convicting power, which impressed the city authorities (4:13). All is ascribed to their being 'filled', as the house where they were was 'filled' with sound like a rush of wind (2:2–4), and as other groups were said to have been 'filled' with awe, fear, or fury (*Luke* 5:26; 6:11): the terms suggest a total, overmastering possession by the Spirit. When such a 'filling' by the Spirit is repeated a little later, its sign is again that 'they spoke the word of God with boldness' (4:31, cf 4:8). Appropriately, the outward signs that heralded the Pentecostal miracle were 'the rushing, mighty wind', the familiar symbol, and indeed the name ('breath') of the Spirit in the Old Testament; and the tongues of flame, symbolising the burning speech of inspired men. The following incident, likewise, resembles a typical prophetic sign, a deed of power witnessing to divine authority, and symbolising also the promise of 'saving health' (the original connotation of 'salvation' in Hebrew thought) made in the gospel.

The gift of the Spirit to all who repent, are baptised, and call on the name of the Lord (2:38, 39) will authenticate the truth of Peter's preaching, as throughout *Acts* the Spirit will confirm the word with signs following. At Samaria, the signs and great miracles were evidence of the presence and power of the Spirit (8:13), attesting the message; so impressive was this display, that a former magician, recognising a greater miracle-working than he himself commanded, offered to buy the enduement of the Spirit—and received a severe rebuke (8:18–24). The point of the story, for Luke, appears to be the public acknowledgement, from such a source, of the superior power of the Spirit. But the Spirit is not only a divine Witness beside the witnessing apostles (5:32), he confirms also new converts in their incipient faith, as at Samaria (8:15, 17), and in the specially important case of Cornelius, when the gospel was first preached to a Gentile (10:44–46; 11:12–17). Confirmation by judgement on those who resist, is illustrated in the temporary blindness of Elymas the magician (13:9, 12). As Peter later explained to the Jerusalem council of the Church, the confirmation of the preaching of the gospel to Gentiles consisted exactly in this, that the Spirit was given to them, as to the first apostles—probably a renewed appeal to the example of Cornelius (15:8).

This witness of the Spirit to the gospel with great power and conviction, as described in *Acts*, is remarkably close in meaning to the Johannine promise of the Spirit who should convict the world of sin, righteousness, and judgement. Along with the endowment of prophecy, the boldness to confront men, the eloquence to persuade, and even the language in which to be understood, it comprises a complete solution to one major problem of the first days of the church, the ability to communicate with the unbelieving world.

A great scholar once declared that the first work of the Spirit was fellowship, the creation of community. Without arguing precise priorities, we may accept the emphasis, and note that the next manifestation of the Spirit which Luke mentions is the welding of that 'one accord in one place' into 'one heart and one soul' as another evidence of the 'filling' of the Spirit (4:31,

32). For converts thrust out of their families, or losing their inheritance, the need was urgent, and the generosity created by the Spirit found expression in a voluntary sharing of goods, so that 'all who believed were together and had all things in common; and they sold their possessions and goods and distributed them to all, as any had need', with great hospitality, gladness, and generosity (2: 44–46). Luke repeats that 'no one said that any of the things which he possessed was his own, but they had everything in common . . .'; as a result 'there was not a needy person among them . . .' (4:32, 34):

This 'fellowship of the Holy Spirit' becomes a dominant theme of the New Testament, and Luke gives it great prominence. One incident illustrates both its power and its danger. The generosity of some richer members in sharing possessions with the poorer members, both alike living thereafter on the church's bounty, enticed two—Ananias and his wife, Sapphira —to attempt deliberate fraud. They sold their possessions but secretly held back part of the price received, so that they too could receive of the generosity of fellow-Christians without actually needing to do so. This was a deliberate theft from the Christian community, but because that community was the fellowship of the Spirit, indwelt by the Spirit, the fraud involved also an attempt to 'lie to the Holy Spirit', a conspiracy to 'tempt the Spirit of the Lord'. So closely was the community of Christians identified with the Spirit who had brought it into being. In the event, the judgement visited upon the action was so severe that 'great fear came upon the whole church, and upon all who heard of these things' (5:1–11).

Those saved by the Spirit's witness were added, day

by day, to this Spirit-filled community (2:46, 47); by the gift of the Spirit, the converts in Samaria are confirmed in their membership (8:15, 17), and by the same means the acceptance of Cornelius was made plain to Peter (10:44–48). When in consequence of these steps, and of Paul's mission to the Gentile world, a church council was called to decide upon the terms of Gentile membership, the decision was framed in the words, 'it has seemed good to the Holy Spirit and to us . . .' (15:28). This phrase is not at all exaggerated: it was the Spirit's community into which the Gentiles were being admitted; the church believed she was guided by the Spirit in so doing; and what was implied in the decision was nothing less than Christianity's ultimate break with Judaism and her birth as a world faith.

What comes to consciousness here is the superintendence of the Spirit within the Spirit-filled church. It is seen also at Antioch, when the members, prophets and teachers assembled for worship are instructed to set apart for the Spirit Barnabas and Saul for work to which the Spirit calls them (13:1, 2). It is seen repeatedly, as Peter is prepared by the Spirit, much against his inclination, to receive the messengers from Cornelius (10: 9–23, especially 19)—as when the gift of the Spirit to Cornelius later settles the question at issue, beyond further discussion (10:44; 11:2f, 15–18). The superintendence of the Spirit is evident again when Paul is prevented from initiating work in Asia, and Bithynia (16:6, 7). Much later, Paul's fateful decision to leave Ephesus for Jerusalem (where he was arrested) was taken 'in the Spirit' (19:21), and carried through 'bound in the Spirit' (20:22) despite the Spirit's warnings of the cost to be faced, in suffering and danger (20:23, repeated at 21:4 and 11). The whole mission continued as it began, 'sent out by the Holy Spirit' (13:4).

It may be fanciful, though it is certainly tempting, to see here the real significance of that strange story of the election of Matthias to take the place of Judas in the apostolic band. The use of the lot, never repeated in *Acts*, and the choice of the man, never again heard of, are so puzzling, that an intended contrast with how things were done *after* Pentecost, with the Spirit in charge, *might* be the reason behind the record (1:15f). At all events, the impression given by *Acts* is of a closely-knit group of disciples, at differing stages of spiritual development, at first somewhat at sixes and sevens but quickly unified in mind and spirit by a glowing experience, and then by the over-ruling, governing direction of the Spirit. Very soon, therefore, that Spirit-led community was strong enough, both to withstand great pressure from without, and to expand far beyond Palestine and at considerable speed.

Resilience under persecution and outreach into new areas are two consequences of the superintendence of the Spirit in that infant church: a third is the constant upbuilding of Christians by encouragement, comfort, and joy. The praise that was kindled at Pentecost (2:47; 3:8, 9) resounded at the second in-filling with the Spirit in the great prayer of 4:23f; to great power and great grace (4:33) was added great joy in being counted worthy to suffer dishonour for the name (5:41). With the conversion of their arch tormentor, Paul, the Christians enjoyed a period of peace, 'walking in the fear of the Lord and in the comfort of the Holy Spirit' (9:31). At Antioch in Pisidia, in face of strong hostility, the newly-won converts (and doubtless the evangelists too) 'were filled with joy and with the Holy Spirit' (13:52). So obvious was this emotional tone of the Spirit-endowed life, in its joy and courage, its praise and boldness, that when Paul met a dozen 'disciples' at Ephesus whose manner and mood evidently lacked what Christians should possess, he asked them—not as we might have done, 'What on earth is the matter with you?' but, 'Did you receive the Holy Spirit when you believed?' Receiving answer that they had never heard even that there is a Holy Spirit, Paul instructed, baptised and laid his hands upon them, and 'the Holy Spirit came on them; and they spoke with tongues and prophesied' (19:1–7).

If the gift of communication was the more spectacular and dramatic equipment given to the early church for its immense task, the creation of such a fellowship was at least as important, if the work was to progress and endure. Organisation was at a minimum, but cohesiveness, mutual loyalty, power of corporate decision, joint action and united resistance, rapidly made of the unpromising materials a church that in the end Rome herself could not halt, nor crush. Within that unique community, young converts, Jewish or Gentile, rejected by their families and circles because of their adherence to Christ, found a new family, a close-supporting circle, in which to shelter, learn, grow strong, mature, rejoice, and work for God. We scarcely realise even yet what a miracle of the Spirit the church really is.

But Luke would have us notice, too, that the agents and leaders of this Spirit-filled community were themselves—expressly and explicitly—'men of the Spirit'. It is so said not only of the first nucleus of the church (2:4) and of Peter at Pentecost and later (4:8), and yet again of John and 'their friends' (4:23, 31), it is asserted of Philip the evangelist, directed by the Spirit into the desert to convert the eunuch from Ethiopia, and then directed onwards to Azotus (8:29, 39). The same is asserted of Agabus and his fellow-prophets (11:28), while the elders of the church at Ephesus are reminded that they were appointed guardians of God's flock by the Holy Spirit himself (20:28).

Paul doubtless possessed special advantages for leadership, in his background, personal ability and training, but *Acts* leaves us in no doubt that all he possessed was taken up, sanctified, empowered, when Paul was 'filled with the Holy Spirit'—and not once only (9:17; 13:9). Luke's meaning here must not be evaded, however much in our day we come to prize ability, education, scholarship. If it is wonderful, and an inspiration to us, that 'uneducated, common men' could by the filling of the Spirit shake the city of Jerusalem and reduce the authorities to silence (4:13f), it is equally important, and a warning to us, that an educated, and very uncommon man like Paul, naturally gifted beyond most men and 'advanced . . . beyond many' of his own age as a student of religion (*Galatians* 1:14) *needs no less* that same filling of the Spirit if he is to become leader and spokesman of the Spirit-filled church. God makes use of cleverness and expertise: cleverness and expertise can never make use of God.

Luke says much the same concerning Stephen, eloquent apologist for the gospel and first of all the Christian martyrs. Chosen as a deacon-almoner among 'men of good repute, full of the Spirit and of wisdom' (6:3), and himself 'a man full of faith and of the Holy Spirit' (6:5), his service was extended; 'full of grace and power' he 'did great wonders and signs among the people', which provoked certain Jewish leaders to dispute with him. They 'could not resist the wisdom and the Spirit' (*NEB*: 'inspired wisdom') with which he spoke (6:8–10). What the people heard was wisdom, what they saw was a man of fearless spirit; the unseen source of both, Luke intends us to understand, was the Holy Spirit who filled his life, and by whose further 'filling' he was enabled to see the glory of God, with Jesus standing to receive him at the right hand of God, and died in triumph (7:55).

As human ability still needs the Spirit, so does human goodness. Barnabas, one of the greatest Christians in the New Testament, to whom under God the church owed, beside a splendid example of generosity (4:36f), the reception of Paul into the church's fellowship (9:26–28), the recognition that God's hand was at work at Antioch (11:20–24), the emergence of Paul as a teacher and pastor (11:25–26), the pioneering of the first mission to the Gentiles (13:2, note the order of names), and the restoration of Mark, with the mission to Cyprus (15:36–39), was plainly a man of immeasurable value to the early church, for his leadership, his vision, and his great strength of character. The 'nickname' bestowed upon him by his fellow-leaders is a supreme accolade: 'Son of encouragement'. But it is more, for the original phrase is 'son of *paraklesis*' (4:36), which recalls at once the less familiar name for the Holy Spirit which we owe to *John's Gospel*—the *Paraclete*: Encourager, Comforter. There, again, lay the secret of Barnabas' ministry to his brethren. He is the only man described in the New Testament as 'a good man', and all we read of him suggests largeness of heart, great strength of principle, complete loyalty to others, but especially to those in need of friends—like Paul, and Mark. Yet goodness, like cleverness, is not enough to make a man an agent of the Spirit-indwelt community. So Luke completes his description: 'he was a good man, full of the Holy Spirit and of faith' (11:24).

By such men, with their varied gifts and capacities, and by their co-operation one with another, the early church was led into the understanding and fulfilment of God's purposes for that age. By divine choice and enabling they became efficient for God beyond their personal abilities, with a power for good greater than their own. For an indwelt 'community' can only mean indwelt individuals: and leadership in such a group means yourself *being led* by the Spirit of Christ.

Such is Luke's solution to the immensity of the church's task in that first generation: a promise of the Spirit, to make the whole enterprise credible; a gift for communicating, by universalising the Spirit of prophecy among very ordinary followers of Christ, with a Spirit-vindicated message to proclaim; a Spirit-indwelt community, united in generous mutual concern, continually enlarged by Spirit-won converts, superintended at every point by the Spirit's direction, thrust outward by the Spirit's inspiration, upheld and encouraged by the Spirit's ministry; and Spirit-filled men to lead, to teach and to inspire. This is the central message of *Acts*: the demands of the church's work in the world pose for ordinary men insoluble problems, to which the answer is—the Spirit.

CHAPTER FOUR

'Explaining' Christ

Of course no one truly *explains* Christ, however hard he tries. But it was soon necessary to make clear to new converts, and to strangers to the story, just who Christ was, and to express the meaning of his life and death in language they could understand. Luke has preserved for us one excellent, and evidently well-known, summary of the essential point: 'You know the word which God sent to Israel, preaching good news of peace by Jesus Christ (he is Lord of all), the word which was proclaimed throughout all Judea, beginning from Galilee after the baptism which John preached: *how God anointed Jesus of Nazareth with the Holy Spirit and with power; how he went about doing good and healing all that were oppressed by the devil, for God was with him*'—adding the necessary references to his death and resurrection, to the command to preach, and to the offer of forgiveness (*Acts* 10:37f). If we add to that succinct description the promise which Luke preserves in its Christian depth of meaning: '*He will baptise you with the Holy Spirit* and with fire' (*Luke* 3:16; *Matthew* 3:11; *Mark* 1:8), we possess Luke's own clues to his interpretation of Jesus, as bearer, and bestower, of the Holy Spirit.

Although the events recorded in the Gospels occurred before those related in *Acts*, the writing down took place some thirty (*Mark*) and fifty years later (*Matthew, Luke*). Inevitably, the events were seen in review, in the light of the church's later experience, when much that at the time was puzzling, even heart-breaking (*Luke* 24:13–24), had become transfigured by the glory of the resurrection and ascension; equally inevitably, the meaning of the whole story could now be re-interpreted by Pentecost, and the rich ongoing experience of life in the Spirit. If then words were needed to make clear to a new generation the greatness and power of Jesus, what more natural than for apostles to interpret his story in the light of their own; or for Luke—who tells so movingly of the coming of the Spirit upon the church—to look back also to Jesus as the Spirit-filled Christ, giver of the Spirit?

Not that Luke wrote to resolve any such question about Jesus; *or that this is his only assessment of the Master*. Luke says he wrote that cultured and thoughtful enquirers (or converts) like 'His Excellency Theophilus' might have a researched and connected account of the things surely believed among Christians (1:1–4). Where Mark and Matthew make statements, Luke for such an audience seeks to explain and make persuasive; and among his explanations of Jesus, by hindsight and a post-Pentecost viewpoint, is this representation of Jesus 'anointed with the Holy Spirit and with power', and promising to 'baptise with the Holy Spirit' those who follow him.

This is but one aspect of Luke's picture, the one directly relevant to our theme, but it is surprising how thoroughly Luke underlines it. Luke sees the whole Christian movement, from its earliest beginning in John and from the conception of Jesus in the womb, to the ascension and afterwards, as inspired, governed, and empowered by the Holy Spirit. It began with the announcement of the coming birth of John, who in order to go 'before' the Lord was to be 'filled with the Holy Spirit from his mother's womb' (1:15). At his birth, his father Zechariah was also 'filled with the Holy Spirit', and hailed John as 'the prophet of the Most High' (1:67, 76). Christ's own birth, likewise, Luke ascribes to the action of the Holy Spirit: the angel said to Mary,

> The Holy Spirit will come upon you,
> and the power of the Most High will overshadow you;
> therefore the child to be born will be called holy,
> the Son of God (1:35).

Matthew declares the birth of Christ of a virgin, 'found to be with child of the Holy Spirit', and Joseph is told 'that which is conceived in her is of the Holy Spirit' (*Matthew* 1:18, 20). Luke 'explains' how it will happen, incidentally identifying the Spirit with the 'Power from on high'. This description of the Spirit might come more naturally to a Gentile's mind than to Matthew's, with the Old Testament teaching on the Spirit behind him: at any rate Luke will repeat it, more than once (compare *Luke* 5:17; 24:49; *Acts* 10:38). (The same difference of background may explain why Matthew and Mark speak of David, in calling the Messiah 'Lord' as 'inspired by the (Holy) Spirit', but Luke says that David said it 'himself' (*Matthew* 22:43; *Mark* 12:36; *Luke* 20:42).)

Luke shows the infant Christ surrounded by people themselves filled with the Spirit. Not only John, the forerunner, but Elisabeth, Mary's kinswoman, is filled with the Spirit to congratulate Mary. Later when the babe was brought to Jerusalem to be presented to the Lord, a righteous and devout old man named Simeon, of whom it was said that 'the Holy Spirit was upon him', and to whom it had been 'revealed . . . by the Holy Spirit that he should not see death before he had seen the Lord's Christ', came—again by the inspiration of the Spirit—into the Temple as Jesus was brought in, and he blessed the child, and his mother. Though the Spirit is not expressly named in the next incident, there is little doubt that in calling Anna 'a prophetess' and recording that she also blessed God upon sight of Jesus, Luke means to include her in this highly significant group of Spirit-led, Spirit-filled people who recognised and welcomed the Spirit-born Christ from the beginning (1:39f; 2:25, 26, 27, 36f).

Almost at once, Luke passes to the story of Christ's receiving the Spirit at his baptism: 'When all the people were baptised, and when Jesus also had been baptised and was praying, the heaven was opened, and the Holy Spirit descended upon him in bodily form, as a dove, and a voice came from heaven, "Thou art my beloved Son; with thee I am well pleased" ' (*Luke* 3:21, 22; *Matthew* 3:16f; *Mark* 1:10). Luke could scarcely emphasise more firmly the importance of such endowment, that even one conceived and born 'of the Holy Spirit' should need such added bestowal. The moment marked for Jesus the beginning of public life, and we are probably right to see in the 'bodily form as a dove' an echo of the Spirit brooding like a bird above the abyss at the creative moment at the beginning of the world.

Before describing what the descent of the Spirit brought to Jesus at this time, Luke shows how he returned from the Jordan 'full of the Holy Spirit', was 'led by the Spirit for forty days in the wilderness, tempted', and then 'returned in the power of the Spirit into Galilee' (4:1, 14; *Matthew* 4:1; *Mark* 1:12). This again is a remarkable insistence on the guiding of Jesus' life, step by step, by the Spirit, the more so when slight changes from Mark's account are observed. Mark said Jesus was 'driven' by the Spirit into the wilderness, but Luke says Jesus was 'led'—co-operating freely. Mark says Jesus was tested for forty days, Luke that he was led by the Spirit for forty days, being tested—the slight rephrasing drawing attention rather to the presence of the Spirit than to the pressure of Satan. For Luke, the Spirit filled Jesus as he came to his testing, led him throughout, filled him still as he returned, vindicated, in the power of the Spirit, into Galilee.

The first manifestation of the new endowment which Luke mentions concerns Jesus' wide fame 'throughout all the surrounding country' as he 'taught in their synagogues, being glorified of all' (4:14, 15). The Spirit has evidently endowed Christ with eloquence and teaching-power. At once Luke elaborates this with the story of Christ's return to Nazareth where, invited to share the conduct of worship, he takes up Isaiah and reads:

The Spirit of the Lord is upon me,
because he has anointed me to preach good news
    to the poor.
He has sent me to proclaim release to the captives
and recovering of sight to the blind,
to set at liberty those who are oppressed,
to proclaim the acceptable year of the Lord.

Sitting down, he offered the startling comment, 'This day is this scripture fulfilled in your hearing' (4:18–21). (Matthew has an almost equivalent quotation, at another point, describing Jesus as the Servant of the Lord, upon whom God will put his Spirit to proclaim justice to the Gentiles: *Matthew* 12:18.)

Here, as in *Acts*, the coming of the Spirit is closely linked with 'anointing to preach . . . to proclaim . . . to proclaim' as a Spirit of communication and of prophecy; but, as the following stories soon reveal, actual release of captives, recovery of sight, and setting souls at liberty, are also implied. This double enduement by the Spirit (at birth and in baptism) is for Luke the sufficient explanation of his power to proclaim and his power to perform, and of all the ministry that followed. It is surprising, therefore, that where Matthew shows Jesus speaking of casting out demons 'by the Spirit of God' Luke has the phrase 'by the finger of God' (*Matthew* 12:28; *Luke* 11:20): perhaps we should see in Luke's expression only a vivid metaphor for what Matthew records more simply— and a metaphor recalling the awe of Pharaoh's magicians at the plagues upon Egypt (*Exodus* 8:19), as something new, fearful, inexplicable. The moving of the Spirit in the ministry of Jesus resembled a divine finger stirring that generation to new excitement and expectancy.

As the ministry proceeds, amidst opposition and success, Luke is careful to show Jesus not only striving for men against evil but also 'rejoicing in the Holy Spirit' (10:21), sharing in precisely that joy and exultation of spirit which in *Acts* is so often the sign that disciples are 'filled with the Spirit'. The remaining reference in Luke's gospel to the Spirit as relating to

Jesus is among the most puzzling passages in the New Testament. 'Every one who speaks a word against the Son of man will be forgiven; but he who blasphemes against the Holy Spirit will not be forgiven' (12:10; compare *Matthew* 12:32; *Mark* 3:28, 29). The general meaning of the passage, in the context in which Mark gives it, suggests that the 'blasphemy' which places a man beyond forgiveness is that soul-blindness which does in truth place him beyond repentance, the blindness that can accuse Jesus of working for Satan, can so confuse light with darkness, good with evil, as to call Christ Beelzebul. So long as a man is in that state of moral madness, all straight-thinking, self-understanding, correction, repentance, and so all forgiveness, are necessarily out of reach. Mark explains the warning in exactly this way: 'for, they said, he has an unclean spirit' (*Mark* 3:30).

The question remains, why speaking a word against the Son of man will be forgiven, but he who blasphemes against the Holy Spirit will not be forgiven? Some have suggested that opposition to the 'meek and lowly' Jesus, in the days of his humiliation, is excusable, at least more understandable, than opposition to the testimony of the apostles after the resurrection in the power of the Spirit. That is just possibly the meaning, though it reads much into Jesus' words. Others, noting the change from Mark's 'all sins will be forgiven *the sons of men*' into Luke's 'everyone who speaks a word against *the Son of man* will be forgiven', wonder if sometime during the years before the writing of the gospels the saying has been differently reported by oral witnesses. What seems beyond doubt is that Luke thought of the Spirit as manifesting through Jesus (and later through the disciples, 12:12) such authority and power that to gainsay it was to incur eternal peril.

If now we look back upon the way Luke has introduced Jesus to us, we cannot miss the sequence of mounting affirmations: the preparation of the forerunner by the Spirit, the conception of Jesus by the Spirit, the welcomes and exultation surrounding his birth from people filled with the Spirit, his own enduement at baptism with the Spirit, his prolonged experience of the Spirit during forty preparatory days, including the temptation, and his return in the power of the Spirit to Galilee; the proclamation in the Nazareth sermon of his having been anointed with the Spirit, and the manifestation of the Spirit in power, in his preaching, miracles, personal joy, and conflict with evil spirits. All this cannot be accidental: Luke is interpreting Christ in the light of the later Pentecostal experience, as he who bears the Holy Spirit, without measure.

This is confirmed, to some extent, by the second theme of Luke's gospel concerning the Spirit: the disciples' share in the same experience. Even before the Spirit descends upon Jesus at baptism, the great promise is repeated, which occupies so large a space in the New Testament: John says 'I baptise you with water; but . . . he will baptise you with the Holy Spirit and with fire' (3:16). Matthew records these words (3: 11), so does Mark (1:8); *Acts* 1:5 shows Jesus repeating them; *Acts* 11:16 shows Peter repeating them. It is not hard to see the same meaning underlying *Acts* 19:4 and what followed—Paul begins the saying, varies it, and then acts on the original promise. In John's gospel, the saying is split between 1:26 and 1:33, but only so as to emphasise its importance; and when Matthew records the commission of Christ to make disciples of all nations, he adds to the description of baptism a phrase which must look back to the promise of John at the beginning—'baptising them in the name of the Father, and of the Son, *and of the Holy Spirit*' (28:19). Of six clear, and two merely possible, allusions to this promise, Luke records three clear and one possible— so important is it in his eyes.

Full discussion of the implications here would range far afield. It is certain that John admitted the insufficiency of his own baptism, expressing self-purification by repentance and seeking the divine purification of remission, compared with the total cleansing which Messiah would effect—by fire and Spirit. Jesus said as much to Nicodemus: 'Unless one is born of water *and the Spirit*, he cannot enter the kingdom of God' (*John* 3:5). We seem compelled to understand John's words in their historical context, as a *warning* that if repentance be refused, the imminent Messiah would purify the nation's outward life and institutions by 'fire' (as his flail, shovel, axe and flame sufficiently make clear), and the nation's inner life by 'the spirit of judgement and of burning' (*Isaiah* 4:4; compare *Malachi* 3:2, 3; 4:1). Preaching before the ministry of Jesus had even begun, before Christ's own teaching on the Spirit, before his death and resurrection, John could hardly mean by the Holy Spirit all that Christians came to understand: the confession of his own disciples long afterwards, that they had not 'even heard that there is a Holy Spirit' confirms this (*Acts* 19:3).

For all that, from the repetition of the saying in the church, it is equally clear that Christians came to see the words, by hindsight, as a *promise*, and one that linked the gift of the Spirit *somehow* with the Christian baptism which would replace John's rite (compare *Matthew* 3:16; *Acts* 2:38; 19:2–6; *1 Corinthians* 6:11; 12:13; *John* 3:5; *Titus* 3:5). And their deepest, all-sufficient reason for so understanding John was that this certainly had happened in their experience: Jesus *had* brought to them, placed within their reach, 'participation in the Spirit'. To describe what had happened to themselves, they used John's phrase 'baptised in (or with) the Holy Spirit'.

How central this gift of the Spirit was to Luke's thought about salvation, may be illustrated (not demonstrated) from one or two other passages of his gospel. One is Luke's curious variation of the wording of the great promise with which Jesus encouraged disciples to pray. According to Matthew (7:7–11), Jesus urged that we ask, seek, knock, in the firm assurance that we shall receive, find, discover open doors: and that we rest this confidence on the fact that God is incomparably more trustworthy than any human father—following with the strong question: 'If you then, who are evil, know how to give good gifts to your children, how much more will your Father who is in heaven give good things to those who ask him?' All this Luke reproduces, except for the single variation 'how much more will the heavenly Father give the Holy Spirit to those who ask him?' (*Matthew* 7:7–12; *Luke* 11:9–13). Whatever explanation be preferred of this curious difference of record, it can be agreed that Luke found this version attractive, and important to preserve, because it accords so closely with his own valuation of the Spirit as the greatest of all the gifts purchased for us by the redemptive life and death of Jesus.

Tentatively, it is possible to see the great importance of the gift of the Spirit, as conceived in that demon-ridden culture, emphasised again in the juxtaposition of ideas in *Luke* 11:14–26, the next paragraph. In reply to the charge that he casts out demons by the prince of demons, Christ speaks of himself as stronger than 'a strong man, armed, guarding his palace', of overcoming him, taking away his armour, dividing his spoil—evidently, by exorcism. But this is followed in turn by the story of the unclean spirit which, having gone out of a man, passes through waterless places seeking rest, but finding none, returns and 'brings seven other spirits more evil than himself, and they enter and dwell there; and the last state of that man becomes worse than the first.' The reason for this tragic re-invasion appears to be that the evil spirit finds the house swept and put in order, but untenanted, vacant, and therefore open to re-occupation. The meaning can only be that exorcism, like repentance, is not enough: into the vacuum left by the expulsion of evil must come the Holy Spirit of good—lest the last state be worse than the first.

How the Spirit will manifest himself within believers, according to Luke's gospel, corresponds (as we would expect) with his manifestation in Christ and with the story of *Acts*: 'the Holy Spirit will teach you in that very hour what you ought to say' (12:12). Taken with 21:14, 15, 'Settle it therefore in your minds, not to meditate beforehand how to answer; for I will give you a mouth and wisdom, which none of your adversaries will be able to withstand or contradict', these words recall *Matthew* 10:19, 20 (*Mark* 13:11): 'When they deliver you up, do not be anxious how you are to speak or what you are to say; for what you are to say will be given you in that hour; for it is not you who speak, but the Spirit of your Father speaking through you.' Words so repeated were obviously of great importance to those who so fully treasured them.

Here, as in *Acts*, the Spirit is to be the answer to the problem of communication: the context foreseen is persecution, the disciples being brought before synagogues, rulers, authorities, kings, governors for Christ's sake, though it is added 'this will be a time for you to bear testimony' (21:13). The Spirit who was seen in Jesus to confer eloquence and authority for the preaching ministry in Galilee, will reveal himself in the disciples also as the skilled advocate, the counsel for the defence, pleading their case with the world, and with the adversaries. We think at once of Peter and John before the Sanhedrin, of Stephen before the mob, of the great promise of the Paraclete [Advocate] in John's gospel. The Spirit shall, by God's prevision and care, both speak through the disciples in their testimony and speak for them in their danger. Henceforth, they will never work, or suffer, alone.

And so Luke's first volume closes in urgent anticipation: 'You are witnesses of these things. And behold, I send the promise of my Father upon you; but stay in the city, until you are clothed with power from on high' (24:48, 49). The story of Pentecost, and the whole *Acts* adventure of the Spirit-filled, Spirit-led, Spirit-empowered church, is the sequel. 'Until you are clothed with power from on high' corresponds in the disciples' experience with 'The Holy Spirit will come upon you and the power of the Most High will overshadow you' in Mary's experience, with which the story began. Looking backward, Luke sees the life and ministry of Jesus as all of a piece with the Christians' own experience: as God had 'anointed Jesus of Nazareth with the Holy Spirit and with power' so he anointed also the church. God entered the world in Christ, and continued with men by the Spirit, that the world might be delivered from the power of evil spirits by the truth and power of the only *Holy* Spirit— that is Luke's gospel: the opening of the prison house and deliverance of the captives, by the Spirit-born, Spirit-endowed, Messiah.

It is no insufficient or superficial assessment of Jesus that is implied: Jesus is Son of God, Son of the Most High, Son of man, Son of David, the Beloved, the Chosen, the Holy One of God, the Lord, the Lord's Christ, the Saviour, a great Prophet, the Servant and the King. But the more theological interpretation of Jesus is all the more impressive, all the more relevant, for being kept close to the Christian's daily experience, in the 'explanation' of Jesus as bearer and bestower of the Spirit by whom Christians live and by whom the church is indwelt from age to age.

By the same token, Luke's emphasis contributes greatly to Christian understanding of the Spirit, too. The great lesson here, as in Paul, and in John, is the *personalising* of the Spirit in the thought of men. No longer is the Spirit merely a breath, a pressure, an invisible force or power or 'inspiration', a divine 'influence'. He is so closely associated with Christ as to be, henceforth, 'the Spirit of Christ', 'the Spirit of the Lord', and once, 'the Spirit of Jesus' (*Acts* 16:7). An expression like 'Father, into thy hands I commit my spirit' (*Luke* 23:46) warns us against supposing that

Luke identifies the person of the Spirit with the person of Christ. But for all that, Luke takes great care that, for all time, men shall recognise and know the Spirit of God as he who endowed Jesus for ministry, and now endows the church with the mind and character of her Lord.

So, on the one hand, with Luke's work before us, the church can never again descend to a notion of the Holy Spirit as the divine magician, the worker of tricks, the purveyor of wonders and signs and provider of thrills; or as an impersonal 'spiritual power' that none can explain but which certain privileged, or skilled, or 'charismatic' Christians can learn to manipulate—all this is exposed as sub-Christian by Luke's portrait of the Spirit-born, Spirit-led, Spirit-endowed, and Spirit-filled Jesus. On the other hand, if we ask just what made Jesus different, and what he obtained for us by his life and death and resurrection, to both questions Luke's answer is—the Spirit.

CHAPTER FIVE

The future

Of nineteen clear references, in John's gospel, to the Holy Spirit, no less than fourteen have to do directly with the approaching departure of Christ. This, plainly, is *the* problem-situation faced in John's teaching on the Spirit, recording Christ's thought: the disciples' fear of a threatening future without Jesus in their company.

Passing by the more debateable uses of the word 'spirit' (3:6; 4:23, 24; 6:63; 11:33; 13:21), we may note the Baptist's testimony, 'I saw the Spirit descend as a dove from heaven, and it remained on him. I myself did not know him; but he who sent me to baptise with water said to me, "He on whom you see the Spirit descend and remain, this is he who baptises with the Holy Spirit." And I have seen and have borne witness that this is the Son of God' (1:32–34): this echoes exactly Luke's teaching that Jesus is bearer and bestower of the Spirit, as well as Son of God. The evangelist's own testimony, 'He whom God has sent utters the words of God, for it is not by measure that he gives the Spirit; the Father loves the Son, and has given all things into his hand' (3:34, 35), probably recalls Isaiah's prophecy that the Spirit shall rest upon Messiah, 'the Spirit of wisdom and understanding, of counsel and might, of knowledge and the fear of the Lord'. It is scarcely true that 'He whom God has sent' [Jesus] gives the Spirit 'without measure' to believers—an alternative interpretation—while 'the Father . . . has given *all things* into his hand' seems to underline the thought that the Father gives the Spirit without measure to Christ. Christ is so 'filled' with the Spirit of prophecy that his every word is God's; he can therefore safely be 'believed'.

It could hardly be, however, that the Spirit of God should come upon men without radically changing them. John records teaching that describes such a gift of the Spirit as nothing less than a totally new birth; so that those receiving him become thereby inexplicable and unpredictable: the natural characteristics of the wind [breath] mark their life—'you do not know whence it comes or whither it goes'. Those upon whom the Spirit comes are born 'from above' and 'anew' (*John* 3:3, 5–8).

John's analysis of renewal is crucial to our appreciation of the experience of the Spirit. Two levels of living are open to man: the natural level, and that which is above nature, though not alien to it: 'flesh' and 'spirit'. On the natural level, man's limitation of vision and achievement sets bounds to his experience; his initiatives and energies, his goals and motives, are mainly from within himself, and the tendency of his whole life is towards what is material, of the senses, mortal. Wilfulness apart, it could not be otherwise, and because of it man's behaviour is generally foreseeable and explainable—at any rate, by hindsight. He is, we say, just being himself. 'That which is born of the flesh *is* flesh.'

But it is part of the nature of man to be *open to* influences, forces and initiatives that are not his own:

some of them evil, demonic in New Testament terms; and some of them good, holy, divine. Man can become 'possessed'. Possession by the Holy Spirit creates a wholly new self, renewed in nature, impulses, reactions, resources—a totally new personality 'made over' to a new pattern. Born again, from above, he is not to be understood or explained by any of the previously valid character-traits and motives that once made him what he was; he is a new creation—'that which is born of the Spirit is spirit'. Nor can his reactions, initiatives and motives now be predicted with the kind of assurance that once made us say 'I know just what he will say—or do!' Because the new-born personality responds to different stimuli, judges things by different values, is aware of unprecedented motions of the Spirit, and is claimed by altogether new loyalties. His life henceforth appears eccentric to observers, though to another reborn soul all is clear. 'A fresh wind,' his friends will say, 'is blowing through his sails, a wind of change.' It is not the wind, Jesus might reply, but the Spirit of God.

This new dimension of experience differentiates the Christian man from the finest humanist. Within humanist limitations, as Jesus suggested to the cultured Nicodemus, that which is born of human nature remains by nature human. Only that which is born of the supernatural Spirit can see or enter the realm that is above nature, and live by supernatural energies in the kingdom of God. The natural is not excluded; nor is the process magical. By 'unless a man is born of water . . .' Jesus must surely be referring Nicodemus to the message and practice of the Baptist, with its tremendous emphasis upon preparatory repentance, creating the conditions for the imminent Messiah. But the profoundest repentance is still *human*, and can do no more than create the conditions for the divine action by the Spirit in total personal renewal—and even that preparatory repentance, as man will come to see, is itself the work of the Spirit, too. A man must be born therefore of water *and the Spirit* before the supernatural insight ('he cannot *see* . . .') and experience ('he cannot *enter* . . .') that belong to the kingdom are brought within his reach. John has nothing to say about 'gifts' and 'signs' and 'miracles' of the Spirit, except the greatest miracle of all, *a man reborn.*

John's remaining references to the Spirit are among the richest on this theme in the New Testament. Their main intention is set out in 7:39, where to a thirsty world is offered the invitation to come, drink, believe, and find unlimited *refreshment*: 'Jesus stood up and proclaimed, "If any one thirst, let him come to me and drink. He who believes in me, as the scripture has said, 'Out of his heart shall flow rivers of living water'."' Now this he said about the Spirit, which those who believed in him were to receive; for as yet the Spirit had not been given, because Jesus was not yet glorified.' The best comment here is the close parallel in thought in the gracious promise Matthew records: 'Come to me, all who labour and are heavy laden, and I will give you rest. Take my yoke upon you, and learn from me; for I am gentle and lowly in heart, and you will find rest for your souls. For my yoke is easy, and my burden is light' (*Matthew* 11:28–30). Yet in the *Matthew* promise, the refreshment is strictly cessation from labour, recuperating one's own powers; and the means is by carrying the yoked burden Christ's way, with meekness and lowliness of heart. In the promise in John, the refreshment is by inward renewal added to any power one has, and the means is—the Spirit.

Behind the imagery in John lies possibly the great vision of Ezekiel, foreseeing a time when out of the city of God shall flow a river, at first ankle deep, then to the thighs, then waters to swim in, so limitless and ever-increasing shall be the flow of God's grace (*Ezekiel* 47). So shall they find, who come to Christ, and drink. A nearer allusion is to the water poured out in the Temple courtyard at the Feast of Tabernacles, in memory of the water miraculously provided in the desert for the journeying tribes on the way to Canaan. Yet, taken quite literally, the words imply more than receiving refreshment: those who drink of Christ become a source of refreshment to others—'*Out of* his heart shall flow rivers of living water.' In the similar promise given earlier to the woman of Samaria, the water was to become a spring, or well, within the soul, so that whoever drank would never thirst again (4:14); here the spring becomes an out-flowing river, and the refreshed soul a channel for the Spirit into surrounding lives.

For the source of this inward renewal and out-flowing river of life is the Spirit 'which those who believed in Christ were to receive'. But, John insists, *not yet*: 'the Spirit had not been given, because Jesus was not yet glorified' (7:39). The experience of the Spirit must await the departure of Jesus, that turning-point in salvation-history, the death, resurrection and ascension of Christ which John always telescopes into one word: 'glorified'. The new age of the Spirit waits upon the supreme act of sacrifice, unveiling and vindication in which, even more clearly than in the ministry, men should see his glory. Only when Christ has given his life and taken it again, fulfilled the commandment received of the Father, and returned to the glory he had before the world was, only then would the new regime be established, and the Spirit of God—the Spirit of the glorified Christ—be given to all who believe, spring and well and river of a new life.

This is the theme of the teaching on the Spirit which John has preserved: the Spirit is the determining Presence in the age that is to be. The future, without Christ in the flesh, is empty, bewildering, full of fore-boding and of problems, but to each the Spirit is the answer, for each the Spirit is the divine provision. When Christ is glorified, the Spirit will come. As clearly as any passage in the New Testament, John's treasured discourse in the upper room confirms the practical approach to the understanding of the Spirit. Here are five outstanding pronouncements on the coming and ministry of the Spirit, from the lips of Jesus himself, and the context in which they are spoken is a series of urgent, down-to-earth questions about what the disciples will do, how they are to manage, without Christ—

Lord, where are you going?

Lord, why cannot I follow you now?

Lord, we do not know where you are going; how can we know the way?

Lord, how is it you will manifest yourself to us, and not to the world?

What is this that he says to us, 'A little while, and you will not see me, and again a little while, and you will see me;' . . . We do not know what he means.

And among the replies of Jesus:

> Truly, truly, I say to you, one of you will betray me.
> Now is the Son of man glorified . . .
> Yet a little while I am with you . . . You will seek
> me . . . Where I am going you cannot come . . .
> Yet a little while and the world will see me no
> more . . .
> Let not your hearts be troubled, neither let them be
> afraid.
> The ruler of this world is coming . . .
> If the world hates you, know that it hated me . . .
> they will persecute you . . .
> They will put you out of the synagogues; indeed,
> the hour is coming when whoever kills you will
> think he is offering service to God.
> Now I am going . . .
> The hour is coming, indeed it has come, when you
> will be scattered . . . in the world you have
> tribulation . . .

The whole conversation is overshadowed, not only by
Jesus' impending departure, but by the needs and
problems which his absence will create, and especially
by the hostility that awaits them as they face the
future without his leadership and company.

Christ's antidote for this mood of unreadiness and
fear is, in general terms, the assurance that they will
not be left leaderless, 'comfortless': another 'Comforter' will come, who will not depart, but remain with
them for ever. This promise is repeated with unexpected argument: 'It is expedient for you'—actually
better, and to your advantage—'that I go away, for if
I do not go away, the Counsellor will not come to

you; but if I go, I will send him to you' (16:7). The advent of the Spirit is no mere compensation for the loss of Christ's earthly presence: his coming is pure gain, for which even the departure of Christ is not too high a price to pay! No one but Jesus would have urged that consideration.

Nor is that all. This general assurance, that the Spirit will be the answer to all the needs of the future, is broken down in detailed application to specific fears and questions. One question is (and every student, at any rate, will sympathise), 'How shall we possibly remember all that we have seen, and heard, and half-understood?' The answer is the Spirit—'He shall bring all things to your remembrance.' 'How shall we possibly grasp, and understand, all that these things mean?' The answer is the Spirit—'He shall lead you into all truth.' 'But the future must be so different— how shall we find the way forward?' The answer is the Spirit—'He shall show you things to come.' 'Still, understanding apart, how shall we face the world's hostility and hatred?' The answer is the Spirit—'He shall convict the world of sin, and righteousness, and judgement.' 'But even so, how can we survive without the Lord?' The answer is the Spirit—'He shall take of the things that are mine and show them unto you.' 'Yet who will replace Jesus, to whom shall we go?' The answer is the Spirit—'We will come, and make our abode with you . . . He dwelleth with you, and shall be in you . . . I will come to you.'

In that last promise (14:17, 18, 23), we approach as nearly as in any passage of the New Testament to identification of the Spirit with Christ. The 'personali-sation' of the Spirit in human thought is here complete. He is in some sense Christ's other self, *the form of the contemporary Christ in the experience of believers through the ages*, dwelling now within disciples as once he lived beside them, to be for Christians to the end of time, and to the ends of the world, all that Jesus had been to the Twelve in Galilee and Judea. It is not that the disciples will have the presence of the Spirit instead of the company of Christ, but that in having the Spirit they will continue to have the Christ in him.

Partial illustration of the practical meaning of this 'substitution' of the Spirit for the earthly presence of Christ may be seen in one disciple's changeful experience. So long as he was near Jesus, Peter was strong and bold; he confessed Christ's messiahship ahead of all others, leaped from the boat to walk on the water, impulsively but with great courage defended Christ in the garden. Within the hour, Peter and Christ were separated—and a serving-girl could so frighten him that he denied Christ with oaths, and went out weeping bitterly. As soon as Christ, now risen, is 'available' again, Peter is passionately confessing his love and ready to be bound and carried where he would not go; at Pentecost he is his bold, challenging self once more, defying Jerusalem, free of speech, in and out of prison —not now in the presence of the earthly Jesus but filled with the Spirit. 'Another Comforter' was to Peter now all that Christ had been.

The name 'Comforter' hardly conveys today what Jesus meant, though its connection with 'fort', 'fortify' and 'fortitude' once made it a suitable translation. The Greek title, *Paraclete*, has not won acceptance with many Christians, yet it expresses Christ's thought. The 'one called alongside to render assistance' (to 'fortify' someone in need), may be a personal friend testifying to character or providing support; an advocate or counsel ('counsellor'), a defending solicitor, presenting one's case before a court; a Christian brother, or a pastor, offering counsel, friendship and encouragement to a heart in need. The legal, and the pastoral, uses of the word are prominent in the New Testament.

'Advocate', or 'attorney' is used of Jesus in *1 John* 2:1, and the idea of one pleading on behalf of another is used of Jesus again in *Hebrews* 7:25, and of Jesus, and the Spirit, in *Romans* 8:34, 27, in the same context as 'laying [accusations] to the charge of God's elect'. The language recalls the picture in *Job* 2 of an 'adversary', *the Satan* ('the accuser of our brethren'— *Revelation* 12:10), the devil-advocate in person, standing before God to slander Job. The Spirit (and the risen Christ) on the other hand plead the defence before the throne of God. This in turn recalls one of the earliest ways in which the promise of the Spirit is expressed—the defender who will be 'mouth, matter, and wisdom' to those arraigned for their faith before synagogue tribunals or judicial courts (*Matthew* 10:19, 20; *Luke* 21:14, 15). The 'Paraclete' comes alongside in moments of peril to plead the Christian's cause.

The pastoral implication in the word arises from the constant use of the cognate word *paraclesis* for the 'word of exhortation', the counsel, support, encouragement, sometimes restraint, by which one believer 'edifies' another in the warm fellowship of the church (*1 Corinthians* 14:3). It was natural that Barnabas, being full of the Spirit, should be nicknamed by his colleagues 'son of paraclesis' [*son of encouragement*, or, as *NEB*, *son of exhortation*, *Acts* 4:36]. The Paraclete promised in the upper room is the one who, through pastor, or friends, or scripture, or the quiet motions of the heart, brings encouragement, illumination, support or warning, that sees us through the testing hour. So Jesus promised his fearful, bewildered disciples, facing an unknown, and so menacing, future.

Of the five great 'Paraclete promises' which John preserved, the first (14:15–18), prefaced by the condition 'If you love me you will keep my commandments', declares that the Paraclete will be given by the Father at the intercession of Jesus, and will remain for ever. He is the Spirit of truth, available only to those who already see and know him—as the disciples do, for he dwells with them in Christ. His coming will, in fact, be a 'return' of Christ, and his ministry to the disciples will be in the 'intellectual' realm of *truth*. This may explain the pre-condition: only those whose obedient hearts can dwell with truth already, may know the full indwelling of the Spirit of truth.

The second promise defines this 'intellectual' ministry by the Spirit, now 'sent' by the Father 'in Christ's name' as 'teaching all things' and 'bringing to remembrance' all that Christ had said. Both recall and interpretation seem to be implied—as both are certainly needed in Christian life; and the word 'remembrance' links the gift of the Spirit with the institution of the Supper as Christ's twin provisions against forgetfulness. As the Supper roots Christian experience in the past, while rekindling a present devotion, so the Spirit keeps Christian experience living and spontaneous, while testing all innovations by what Jesus said to us (14:26).

The third promise (15:26) speaks of the Paraclete, the Spirit of truth, as 'coming' and 'sent' by Christ from the Father, *proceeding* from the Father—a remarkable group of expressions which manage to show the coming of the Spirit as the united action of

Father, Son and Spirit, 'indistinguishably separate'. His ministry is again 'intellectualist', this time 'bearing witness' alongside the witness of the disciples. Here a ministry towards the outside world is coming into view, though through the disciples, and assisting them to 'answer' for their faith (*Luke* 21:13, 14).

It is part of the character of God, as revealed in scripture, to be constantly in movement towards man —'coming down', 'going forth', 'sending', 'seeking': in modern terms, he is 'the out-going God'. Is it too fanciful to link with that dynamic, forth-reaching grace of God the phrase 'proceedeth from the Father', and think of the Spirit as 'personifying' the out-goingness of God?

The fourth promise elaborates the Spirit's ministry towards the world. The context emphasises Christ's no longer being with the Twelve, His departure to 'him who sent me', and the disciples' consequent sorrow; there follows the assertion that it is better that he goes, in order that the Paraclete might come. But it is towards the world that his ministry will be directed, again as an 'intellectual' ministry of conviction. He will convince the world of what for John is the supreme sin, of not believing the truth, of rejecting light and preferring darkness and ignorance. He will convince the world also of the true nature of righteousness, as Jesus is vindicated in resurrection, glorified in ascension, welcomed by the Father. He will convince the world of the reality of judgement, beginning already, as in the cross both the world (12:31), and the demonic ruler of the world are judged—revealed in true light and destined for condemnation, 'cast out'. The Spirit is given to the church ('send him *to you*'): but his witness operates also upon the conscience of the world, to bring conviction that after all Christ was the truth, the universe is moral, and judgement inexorable (16:7–11).

The fifth promise (16:13–15) reverts to the title 'Spirit of truth' and to the Spirit's ministry to the disciples themselves. It is still described in 'intellectualist' terms—'guide you into all the truth', 'speak', 'hear', 'declare'. New in this promise is an insistence upon the Spirit's own initiative: he no longer is *sent*, or *given*, he *comes*, *will guide*, *hears*, *speaks*, *declares*, *glorifies*, *takes*, in the fullness of personal activity. Equally clear is the Spirit's firm relation to Christ: he will not speak on his own authority, not what he himself would say, but what he hears (? what he is commanded) that he will speak. He will not glorify himself, but only take what belongs to Christ and exhibit, declare it to the church—and this is repeated, with the reminder that all that the Father has is included in what belongs to Christ. And one further new promise here is that the Spirit will take full care of the future, with all its changes. He will prove to be the Spirit of progress—showing to Christ's own 'the things that are to come', leading forward into new circumstances, and into all the truth as yet unspoken (16:12).

It would be folly to miss, in these great utterances, certain far-reaching principles which should govern our thought about the Spirit. For example, the orientation of his ministry towards the world is as clear in *John* as in the early chapters of *Acts*. To concentrate therefore upon the ministry of the Spirit to the Christian, or to the church, whether in spiritual or in spectacular ways, is to narrow the promise of Christ in a way unworthy of his intention, which was (as we said) equipment rather than enjoyment. It would be folly to under-appreciate the relation of the Spirit to Christ in these great sayings: older ideas of a 'power' or 'force' are here completely left behind; the Spirit is Christ's 'other self'. Phrases like 'the Spirit *poured*', '*baptised* with the Spirit', '*having* the Spirit', linger for a long time, even in the New Testament, and sub-personal terms are still common in Christian discussion of the Spirit. Such language may do little harm, if it be not allowed to control our thought of him who is the Spirit of Christ. In the upper room conversation, all our relations with the Spirit are fully personal, and fully passive: he controls us, comes to us, teaches us, leads us—*we never manipulate him.*

It would be folly, again, to miss the emphasis upon his Christ-focused ministry. The church has always felt that any movement, like the early Montanism, which drew especial attention to the ministry of the Spirit, as an end in itself, was in some way out of harmony with the New Testament presentation. The experiments at Corinth tended to confirm this feeling, as do later, and even modern, 'Spirit movements' where all the emphasis falls upon the experience, the gifts, the power, *of the Spirit.* It may be for this reason that the church has never authoritatively defined the doctrine of the Spirit with the thoroughness she gave to the doctrine of Christ. The root of this feeling is doubtless the five-fold insistence of Jesus that the Spirit shall not draw attention to himself, speak of himself, exercise his own authority, glorify himself, or ever declare 'the things of the Spirit'—but only the words, authority, interests and glory of Christ himself. With those clear words in mind, the church has ever suspected that *the Spirit may well be most powerfully present when he is being least talked about.*

And it would be scarcely less folly to miss the way these great promises relate to the problem constantly faced in the later books of the New Testament—the difficulties raised by the 'absence' of Christ. When Jesus spoke, the fear was of his departure; when John was writing, the great anxiety was that he had not returned. Matthew's answer to the complaint 'My Lord delayeth his coming' is 'The end is not yet . . . keep watching!'—and the reminder that the risen Christ is with us always, in the heart of the congregation. *2 Peter*'s answer was to telescope time—a thousand years are with the Lord as one day. John has preserved for us sayings which throw a new light on the problem. Phrases like 'I will not leave you uncomforted, I will come to you . . . A little while and you see me no more: again a little while and you will see me . . . I will come again . . .' have the authentic ring of the advent hope. But 'I go to the Father, and you will see me no more . . . We will come and take up our abode with him . . . He dwells with you and shall be in you . . .' appear to transmute the hope of a *visible* return of Christ into the presence of Christ by the Spirit in the hearts of believers, even as (in part) Matthew had done.

Certainly the hope of some final 'return' of Christ is not lost (5:25–29; 6:39, 40, 44, 54; compare *1 John* 3:2, 3). 'The last day' shines as clear in *John* as anywhere in the New Testament. But the practical difficulty for the church occasioned by the delayed hope is, in these sayings, partly removed, or alleviated, by the strong reminder that the church after all is *not* 'without Christ', even pending the advent. 'He will be in you.'

John records Jesus making one more reference to the Spirit (20:22). It is the evening of Easter day; the doors are shut where the disciples are assembled, but Jesus appears, saying 'Peace be with you', showing them his hands and his side, repeating the benediction of peace, and adding the Johannine form of the great commission: 'As the Father has sent me, even so I send you'. 'And when he had said this, he breathed on them, and said to them, "Receive the Holy Spirit. If you forgive the sins of any, they are forgiven; if you retain the sins of any, they are retained".' To the last, the context in which the gift of the Spirit is mentioned is the departure of Christ; this time, the disciples are to share his own commission, received from the Father, and to continue his work. So they will bear responsibility for removing or retaining the sins of the world —doubtless by offering to men, or failing to offer, the remedy of the gospel. It is with a view to this commission and responsibility that Christ breathes upon them and bids them receive the Spirit—for the future task.

The simplest impression would be that the endowment was received then, in the upper room: there seems little point in mentioning the Lord's 'breathing' upon them (with its echo of the Old Testament and of *John* 3:8—the wind), if the Lord's words are but a promise of Pentecost to come. Some feel, however, that Pentecost is so clearly the *first* enduement of the church by the Spirit, that the Easter day incident can only be prophecy, not actuality. John's insistence that Jesus must depart before the Spirit can come supports this understanding of the text. On either interpretation, the main emphases of John on this theme are here neatly summarised: the very close relation of the

Spirit to Christ—his very breath; the bestowal of the Spirit by Jesus; the entirely practical nature of the gift, as equipment and assurance for the future; and the ultimate beneficiaries (so to speak) of the gift are those to whom the disciples are sent. If the giving and withholding of remission is by preaching, or neglecting to preach, the gospel, then even John's emphasis on the 'intellectualist' ministry of the Spirit—in teaching, remembrance, declaring, convicting—is not here forgotten.

So very much do we owe to John's gospel for the Christian understanding of the Spirit, and his relation to the church's mission. John makes it so abundantly clear that to the unknown and threatening future, to the unreadiness and fears of the church, to the hostility and unbelief of the world, to the sadness of advent hope deferred, Christ's answer is—the Spirit.

CHAPTER SIX

How salvation works

A letter so central to Christian understanding of salvation as the *Epistle to the Romans*, and containing no less than twenty-two clear references to the Holy Spirit, is bound to touch upon, or to anticipate, aspects of the theme more fully expounded elsewhere. At the outset we are reminded of the close relation of the Spirit to Jesus, and the function of the Spirit as witness to the truth, when we read that Christ was 'designated Son of God in power according to the Spirit of holiness by his resurrection from the dead' (1:4). The unusual phrase 'Spirit of holiness' suggests Paul is citing a very early formula for confession of the deity of Christ. The single reference in *Romans* to the sanctifying power of the Spirit—'that the offering of the Gentiles may be acceptable, sanctified by the Holy Spirit' (15:16)—recalls *Thessalonians*, anticipates *1 Corinthians*, and echoes *Acts* 15:9—'God made no distinction between us and them (the Gentiles) but *cleansed* their hearts by faith'. Like Peter, and any other Jew, Paul would feel that anything Gentile was 'unclean': Peter sees Christian Gentiles cleansed by their *faith*, Paul sees them cleansed by the Spirit.

Speaking of the 'signs and wonders' which attested his own mission among the Gentiles, Paul is careful to ascribe all power to the Spirit (15:19). He is similarly careful, protesting his truthfulness in speaking of his love for his own nation, not to appeal to his own conscience merely (any man will do that!), but to his conscience as enlightened and confirmed by the inner assent of the Holy Spirit, a judgement far more searching and authoritative than his own (9:1). The phrase, 'I appeal . . . by *the love of the Spirit*' (15:30) is unique in the New Testament; the nearest parallel is *Colossians* 1:8—'your love in the Spirit'. But the idea that the Spirit is the Creator of fellowship, and of unity, is a main theme of *Acts*, *1 Corinthians*, and *Ephesians*. In several verses, 'spirit' does not refer to the Holy Spirit (1:9; 2:29; 8:10, 16; 11:7); in two the meaning is more doubtful, though it is certain that Paul would trace both 'a spirit of sonship' (8:15) and 'ardour of spirit' (12:11 *NEB*), if these are correct translations, to the work of the Holy Spirit within the Christian heart.

Such incidental references reveal once more how constantly the dependence of the Christian upon the Spirit is present to the apostle's mind. They add little to New Testament teaching; direct instruction about the Spirit is no part of the purpose of Paul's letter. Even the gifts that enable Christians to serve the fellowship are not, in *Romans*, described as 'gifts of the Spirit' (12:6f). All that Paul has to say about the Spirit in this letter, and it is much, arises directly from the letter's main theme: the Christian experience of salvation, and how it works.

Paul defines the letter's purpose very clearly when he announces his intention to visit Rome, and from there to press forward to evangelise Spain and the West. He hopes for the zealous support and material assistance of the church already at Rome, and writes to stimulate that support (1:11–15; 15:23–29). But various rumours and suspicions have preceded him, concerning what exactly he preaches, how his message is related to the faith of the Jewish fathers, how far he remains a loyal Jew or has become a renegade, and especially, is his gospel of salvation by faith alone, without the law, a morally sound, safe, effective message when preached among loose-living pagans? To gain Rome's active interest in his mission, Paul must explain where he stands on points like these, and *Romans* is the result.

Proving from the Old Testament and from general observation the sinfulness of all men, he declares that God has 'set forth Christ', with expiatory power through his death; and through him a salvation to be received by faith, that all may find in place of sinfulness the righteousness offered to those who have faith in Jesus. So far from such 'righteousness through faith' contradicting the faith of the fathers, it was wholly consonant with the experience of Abraham and of David. And it certainly works, bringing peace, access to God's favour, the hope of recapturing the glory lost in Eden, endurance and joy in suffering, so developing character and imparting hope. Such hope would not disappoint, for already, in those counted righteous through their faith, divine love had been poured into their hearts through the Holy Spirit which had been already given to them (5:5).

Thus the Spirit enters the main argument as one of the grounds of assurance that the gospel really does work. The first affirmation concerning him is, that he 'has been given to us'. There is no suggestion of the Spirit's being made 'available', so that we may 'possess the Spirit' or 'be initiated (baptised) with the

Spirit' if we go far enough in faith and consecration: the Spirit *has been* given to us. The point will be placed beyond argument later when Paul lays down its converse as a rule: 'Any one who does not have the Spirit of Christ does not belong to him' (8:9).

The reasonableness of Paul's message is urged by its parallel with the Adam story, and then the real crux of the argument is reached: If a man is saved by faith, apart from obedience to the moral, or the Jewish, law, *why should he not continue in sin*, so that divine grace and forgiveness toward him might be all the greater! Paul's answer has two parts. On the one hand, he expounds 'saving faith' as a union with Christ so close that the convert becomes united with Christ in his death to sin, self, and the world—and can no longer continue therein; and united with Christ in his resurrection, so as to live henceforward in the newness and power of a risen life. By the very 'faith' that saves him, he is dead to sin, alive to God (6:1–11). That gives the clear negative reply to the critic's question: the man made righteous by his faith cannot willingly go on sinning—his faith has made him one with Christ, in dying to sin and in living for God.

But the positive reply is immensely stronger. Having been set free (by death with Christ) from slavery to sin (6:16–18), and also from the law which could not cure sin, only condemn it (7:1–25), the man with faith in Jesus comes under the overmastering rule of 'the Spirit of life in Christ Jesus' (8:2). *That transforms him.* The believer need not go on sinning, for he is free; the moral law could not break the power of sin, but the Spirit does; so, all the requirements and ideals expressed in the divine law can now be fulfilled in us, as we walk, in daily behaviour, not after the dictates and enticements of the flesh, but after the rule and allurements of the Spirit (8:1–4). 'We are discharged from the law, dead to that which held us captive, so that we serve not under the old written code but in the new life of the Spirit' (7:6).

Such is the crucial place of the Spirit in the process of individual salvation. He takes possession of the believing heart, hitherto the slave of sin and under condemnation by the law, and in place of sin and law he directs the believer's life. That, also, is why the Christian cannot continue in sin. Once Paul himself, desperate to earn divine commendation for the righteousness which is 'of the law', after all his effort could only cry 'Wretched man that I am! Who will deliver me from this body of death?' Now he testifies to God's answer in the gospel: 'The law of the Spirit of life in Christ Jesus has set me free from the law of sin and death' (8:2). With this tremendous moral dynamic, the very energy of God the all-holy, the all-good, flowing forth in the divine Spirit, Paul comes to the rescue of the man helpless to redeem himself. Henceforth, he who believes in Jesus is accepted by God, as though he were already righteous, in order that under the rule of the Spirit he might be made actually righteous—'that the just requirement of the law might be fulfilled in us, who walk not according to the flesh but according to the Spirit' (8:4), in the purity, joy, and power of a personal Pentecost. *But how does it work?*

(i)

It involves, Paul says, an explicit reorientation of mental life, a 'set of mind', against things 'fleshly', material, sensual and sinful, and towards 'the things of the Spirit'—the things which the Spirit desires to teach, impart, and cultivate within the Christian. The 'walk', the daily behaviour, will then follow that set of the mind. This reorientation is necessary, because those whose minds are set on the flesh are, in their inmost thought, hostile to God, rejecting even the desire to fulfil God's law, and in any case unable to do so; those absorbed in the things of the flesh cannot please God. It is also blessed: for whereas the result of thought and behaviour obsessed with the flesh is 'death'—the withering of all that is fine, and tender, and pure within the soul—the end-result of thought and behaviour tending always towards the Spirit is life ever refreshed, and peace ever renewed (8:5–8).

Of Christians, Paul can say that this inner reorientation has already taken place: 'You are not in the flesh, you are in the Spirit, if the Spirit of God really dwells in you. Any one who does not have the Spirit of Christ does not belong to him' (8:9). But the phrase, 'who walk not after the flesh but after the Spirit' (8:4) is meant to insist that the turning away from the things of the flesh (which was our first repentance), and the turning towards the things of the Spirit (which was our first faith) *must be maintained*, reiterated, constantly reaffirmed, if the rule of the Spirit of life in Christ Jesus is to be experienced to the full, in life and peace.

(ii)

It is not only the inner mental life and its outward moral expression which is quickened by the Spirit. As a Jew, Paul did not think of man as divided into soul and body, but as a single living being, an 'animated body', with the body as essential to a whole personality as the mind. That is why the predicament with which salvation has to deal is both moral and physical: *sin* and *death*. Because of sin the body is (as good as) 'dead': 'the wages of sin is death', 'death having spread to all men because all men sinned' (8:10; 5:12; 6:23). But already, because of the righteousness found through faith, the believer's spirit knows life, the Spirit makes him really live (8:10). And this experience carries with it, because of the unity of body and soul, the promise and foretaste of immortality. The life which we already experience, the outward nature wasting away while the inward nature is renewed day by day (*2 Corinthians* 4:16), is (as John would say) *eternal* life, life of eternal quality. The Spirit who even now revitalises the inner life, will revitalise also the body, in life everlasting (8:11).

The indwelling of the Spirit in every Christian, imparting life, is once again taken for granted: but two expressions here are striking. Paul passes without warning from 'the Spirit of God . . . dwells in you' to 'if Christ is in you' and back to (God's) 'Spirit . . . dwells in you' as being in experience indistinguishable. But the third phrase is spelled out as 'the Spirit of him who raised Jesus from the dead'—the Spirit of resurrection power, of risen, victorious life. Even so, Paul cannot merely assert as fact what in truth depends on the maintenance of a genuine repentance and faith. As the new orientation towards things of the Spirit must be maintained from day to day, so the experience of life imparted to the spirit already, and guaranteed to the body thereafter, leaves us an obligation. In such a situation, 'we are debtors': not to the flesh, to live according to the flesh, but to the Spirit, by putting to death the habitual deeds of the fleshly body, by the power of the Spirit, in order to maintain the life of the spirit from day to day (8:12, 13). Having once died with Christ, we must continually, insistently, 'reckon ourselves dead', reaffirming our death with Christ; and so having once risen with Christ we continually reaffirm our newness of life by living unto God (6:8–11).

(iii)

The Spirit, however, is not only the Spirit of a new moral dynamic, and of a new resurrection life: he is also the Spirit of Christ, the Son of God. All whose lives are under his direction are therefore likewise sons of God (8:14). This changes the tone of religious experience: 'you did not receive the spirit of slavery to fall back into fear, but you have received the spirit of sonship' (8:15). It also settles all questions of our status: 'When we cry, "Abba, Father"'—the *Our Father*—'it is the Spirit himself bearing witness with our spirit that we are children of God' (8:16). The subtle change from *sonship* to *children* reminds that legal status rests upon spiritual relationship, the possession of like nature. For good measure, possession of the Spirit settles likewise our destiny: 'if children, then heirs, heirs of God and fellow-heirs with Christ' to fullness of life hereafter (8:17). So once more the experience of the Spirit is the deepest ground of hope, not only of immortality but of glory. 'May the God of hope fill you with all joy and peace in believing, so that by the power of the Holy Spirit you may abound in hope' (15:13). The Spirit who delivers from the past, and sustains in the present, no less effectively irradiates the future, nourishing hope and expectation in dark moods and daunting days.

All this follows, according to Paul, from being under the direction of the Spirit of God's Son, as we come to share in the experience of the Son, suffering with him, glorified with him (8:17). That sets the tone, the status and the outcome of Christian life beyond all debate—and the goal. With all this, we have so far only 'first fruits of the Spirit' (8:23).

(iv)

For Paul is far too realistic to imagine that the life in the Spirit which he has been describing is already perfected in any of his readers. The sharing of Christ's sufferings, yes: but his glory? That awaits the consummation of redemption, when all creation will share this liberty of the children of God (8:21). Meanwhile, though, Christians are often weak, imperfect, inadequate for their great destiny, ignorant even how to pray as they ought, buffetted by circumstances and beset with doubt. It is remarkable how the closing verses of this great chapter bring us back to earth, and to the Christian beset with weakness, ignorance, tribulation, distress, persecution, famine, nakedness, peril and sword—and Paul is not dreaming up possible adversities, but reading from his diary. Even more wonderful, then, that Paul's thought on the Spirit returns at the same time to the familiar and comforting concept of the Paraclete called alongside to help us in our weakness, the Advocate-Priest, interceding for the saints, knowing the will of God as well as the weakness of men, and bringing the two together by prayer within us beyond anything we could ourselves express (8:26, 27).

All things, meanwhile, work towards God's goal, and nothing can separate us from God's love. What that goal is, towards which life and the Spirit lead us, follows clearly from his being the Spirit of God's Son. 'For those whom he foreknew he also predestined to be conformed to the image of his Son, in order that he might be the first-born among many brethren', all bearing the family likeness, wrought in us by the Spirit of the elder Brother (8:28, 29).

So men are saved: by the invasive energies of the Spirit of life in Christ Jesus. By faith in what Christ has done, a faith which unites us to Christ in death and resurrection, we come under the rule of the Spirit, who puts to death in us the deeds of the body, quickens our inner life with the life of God, guarantees to us our immortality, lifts us to the experience of divine sonship, assists us in all weakness, and leads us onward towards Christ-likeness. Sin is not only expiated, it is overmastered; death is not only conquered, it is overwhelmed by life.

So Paul replies with force to *contemporary* criticism of his gospel: certainly it works! But not to *ours*—for all this is intensely individualist. Yet Paul never imagined that individual salvation is sufficient, and before his argument is done he expounds the new life under the Spirit's direction as it finds expression in true patriotism (9–11), in church fellowship and service (12), in the state and in society (13), and among Christian brethren (14–15). At one point in that wider exposition, Paul suddenly sets against the trivial disagreements of petty-minded Christians over *minutiae* of Christian behaviour—meats, drinks, and how to spend your holydays—the wide theme of Christ's own vision and teaching, the kingdom of God. This, he roundly declares, *this*—not quarrelling over scruples—is the heart and crown and goal of Christian living: 'righteousness, peace and joy in the Holy Spirit' (14:17). Life put *right*, life at *rest*, life made *radiant*, under the direction, and in the enjoyment, of the Holy Spirit: 'he who thus serves Christ is acceptable to God and approved by men' (14:18).

And at the same time provides the evidence whether salvation works: the answer is the Spirit.

CHAPTER SEVEN

Personal freedom

The problem dealt with in Paul's vehement letter to the Galatians is the danger of Christian freedom. Yet the early church had no doubt whatever that Christ sets men free. Redemption is, by definition, a setting free by ransom; when Christ stood in his home synagogue at Nazareth, declaring that the Spirit was upon him, he immediately described his coming ministry as including release for captives and liberty for the oppressed. He was Christ the Liberator, who promised, 'If the Son shall make you free, you shall be free indeed.' What, then was the problem?

Nowhere in the New Testament is this Christian freedom more fully analysed. As to its quality, Paul insists that ours is not the freedom of rebellion or irresponsibility: we are born free (4:21–5:1); in contrast with the fear and superstition of the ignorant, ours is a freedom of understanding and of faith (2:16–20; 3:22–26); compared with the waywardness of children, ours is the freedom of the mature (3:25–4:7). As to its range, Paul insists that our freedom is sixfold.

Freedom from the curse is basic to all else (3:10–14). In Jewish thought, a curse rested on all who failed to keep the law; it became obvious in anyone socially condemned to hang upon a tree. By becoming

75

involved in the consequences of our wrongdoing, Christ—so Paul will say, borrowing the ancient language unexpectedly—'became a curse for us', so replacing our 'curse' by two infinitely more welcome destinies, blessing and promise. It is not a metaphor we find attractive, but behind it lies the most coveted of all freedoms in the modern world: freedom from the past, from the merciless entail of previous wrong, from 'the irreparableness of actions'.

Freedom from the law is everywhere in *Galatians*. Men committed to Christ are no longer under endless regulations: they have passed from external obligation to internal discipline, from fear of condemnation to love of good for its own sake. Their goodness springs like 'fruit' (5:22) from the happy impulse of a renewed nature—radiant, spontaneous, self-renewing, *above* the law.

Freedom from the flesh is implied in 2:20—'I have been crucified with Christ . . .' and in 5:16, 'Walk by the Spirit, and do not gratify the desires of the flesh': it is stated in 5:24—'Those who belong to Christ Jesus have crucified the flesh with its passions and desires.' Paul remembers the humiliating helplessness of his former nature, the innate compulsions, subconscious drives, unworthy desires, vacillating efforts at self-betterment, all the deposit of previous yieldings and self-mistrust that make a man prisoner of the self he has become. But now the Spirit of life in Christ has set him free: he is a new creation (6:15).

Freedom from man is the theme of 1:1; 1:10–2:14, where Paul defends the independence of his apostleship, and of 4:17, where he warns against those who flatter or cajole for their own ends, The man of conviction and of conscience is liberated from fear and from flattery; he resists the compulsions of the majority, the social pressures that drown personality in conscienceless conformity. Even political freedom is hinted at in 4:24–31, where Abraham's concubine, Hagar, is likened to 'the Jerusalem that now is . . . in slavery'. This can only refer to the Jewish capital, occupied by Roman forces, whereas Christians are citizens of the heavenly Jerusalem, the mother-city of the free. Today we scarcely realise what inward emancipation within a totalitarian society could mean to subject races under Rome.

And spiritual freedom, too, from the present evil age, from the elemental spirits of the universe, and from the world (1:4; 4:3, 8, 9; 6:14), had more dramatic meaning for those convinced that the natural world was subject to demonic forces, and that the time, the age, were pressing upon Christians with Satanic power. There is no deeper bondage than the helpless fatalism which abnegates responsibility, and resigns the world to demonic forces, to some inexorable determinism of history. From that bondage also Christ has set us free, to 'strive, to seek, to find, and not to yield'.

Gospel freedom from the past, moral freedom from the law, psychological freedom from the flesh, social freedom from the fear of man, political freedom from the idolatry of the state, spiritual freedom from the demons and from fate—it is hard to believe we are listening to a Pharisee, an authoritarian to the ends of his phylacteries—until we remember that this is a Pharisee's testimony to Christ.

Galatians is thus an exposition of Paul's great watchword: 'Where the Spirit of the Lord is, there is freedom' (*2 Corinthians* 3:17). Yet, though Paul is certain that freedom is a gift of the gospel, it does raise a problem—the urgent, practical problem of making freedom *safe*. A surfeit of freedom can be fatal. The Greeks saw the danger, and prized freedom within citizenship; the Romans saw it, and prized freedom within discipline. The Jews saw it, and lost the notion of freedom in that of obedience to divine law. Jewish Christians strictly brought up to think of religion in high moral terms, of God as holy and true, of his law as absolute and eternal, shuddered at a proclamation of complete liberty. What would happen to religion, to society, if all law were abrogated, and the divine commandments set aside?

And when Christianity went forth to the Gentile world, how much greater the peril! Pagans, idolaters, loose-living, immoral, unclean—the Gentiles knew nothing (so Jews thought) of real moral discipline. In Galatia, for example, people were passionate, fickle, given to excitement, and impulsive, as Paul's own letter shows. What would happen when such people, living amidst unmentionable temptations, were advised that Christ had set them *free*? What excesses might they not indulge in, what compromises with pagan 'morality' might they not work out, what disgrace to the gospel might not presently result? The somewhat maligned 'Judaists' who troubled Paul's converts in Galatia were after all genuinely concerned for morality and the good name of Christ. Whatever Paul said about liberation in Christ, Christians just could not be encouraged to live as they liked.

It was appropriate that this problem, anticipated by the churches in Samaria and at Antioch, should come to a head in Galatia, the first wholly Gentile mission-field. But in truth the problem is perennial, and inherent in the Christian outlook. Always, it seems, liberty achieved begins to hunger for order and ,authority, which themselves so often provoke protest, revolt, and liberty again. Paul knew the danger as clearly as any man, and preached a Christ who makes men free—within the kingdom where God reigns, where man delights to be bound. He proclaimed a free grace which removes the yoke of Mosaic legalism, but invites to an allegiance equally submissive, towards the Christ of God, whose we are and whom we serve. The paradox is inescapable. Christ saves, without the law, those in whom the law must yet be fulfilled; and sets us free to bind us 'by such vows as 'twere a shame a man should not be bound by'.

The depth of this tension, and the values at stake, are nowhere more thoroughly explored than in this epistle of freedom. For in the very letter which calls us to stand fast in the liberty wherewith Christ has set us free (see 5:1), Paul insists on the necessary limits of Christian freedom! Christian liberty is exercised within a moral world—a man reaps what he sows (6:7), integrity is expected, and men bear their own judgement and responsibility (2:11–14; 5:10; 6:5); the sinful shall not inherit the kingdom (5:21). Self-denial, too, limits freedom—the flesh is crucified, and the life now lived is 'unto him' (2:20). Christ's law limits freedom, the law of love that forbids devouring one another, requires us to bear one another's burdens, restore the fallen, share good things, do good to all men (5:13–15; 6:1–10). Loyalty to the truth limits intellectual freedom—the gospel is no man's to invent, or vary, or pervert as he pleases (1:6–9). And so does vocation to Christ's service—Paul says he was born to apostleship, converted to it, and called to it (1:1, 15, 16), and from that overmastering purpose he found no escape, and sought none.

This seems a formidable list of qualifications with which to safeguard spiritual liberty, yet Christian liberty is Christian, and these limitations merely spell out the loyalties involved in love for Christ. Why then all the vehemence, the turbulence, of this explosive little letter, provoked when other teachers wanted to safeguard Gentile Christian freedom within Jewish rules of circumcision and Mosaic discipline? The answer lies partly in Paul's jealousy over his newly-won converts, for whom he coveted all the liberty Christ had won for them. But it lies partly also in Paul's own experience—for he knew, none better, that the Jewish law meant bondage, the Mosaic system was a yoke neither he nor the fathers could bear; that the law could not save, but only awaken sin and bring condemnation. *He had come that way*, and found freedom only in Christ: he would not look back, nor allow that only by outward constraint could human weakness and wilfulness be controlled.

Paul knew there is another way.

At first sight Paul's letter to Galatia seems almost incoherent as it switches suddenly from argument about the law to how the Christian ought to live: in fact this is the climax of Paul's great contention—*not law*, he says, *but the Spirit, is the rule of Christian life*. This is his final answer to Judaism, and that watchword of his, about where the Spirit is, there is liberty, measures the distance he has travelled from Pharisaism. The crown and consummation of freedom is surrender to the Spirit. The law had proved the way of failure, inward division, and brooding despair: deliverance came with the invasion of the Spirit as the rule of new life. If *Romans* 8 is Paul's finest exposition of the Christian's *experience* of the Spirit, *Galatians* 5–6 is his finest exposition of the *rule* of the Spirit of life in Christ Jesus.

In 5:16, 25 we are bidden *to walk* by the Spirit. The phrase echoes early descriptions of Christianity as 'the Way', recalling yet older Hebrew usage which described man's daily duty, his pilgrimage, the 'way' of the Lord, as his 'walk'. For every Jewish mind, the sufficient definition of that 'way of the Lord' was the *law*, and Paul fully intends the provocative contrast— 'Let us walk *in the Spirit*'. The Christian's steps must be directed from within. As the context shows, Paul has in mind the two chief areas of morality, self-discipline and social relationships: neither *can* be legally imposed—purity, and love, must proceed from the rule of the Spirit within the soul, or not at all.

In 5:18 we are *to be led* by the Spirit—and again the contrast with the Jewish law is evident. For the law was held by Jewish jurists to direct a man's life from birth to death: and Paul means that everything concerning a man's career, his work, friendships, marriage, attitudes, destiny, are all under the Spirit's direction. Neither an infallible church, nor infallible written documents, nor an inherited convention of Christian behaviour, can provide what the truly guided life requires: the Christian's daily code is the leading of an inward living Spirit.

In 5:22–23, the total *harvest* of the Spirit-filled life is described in nine of the loveliest graces of Christian living. Love is the first, and supreme, gift of the Spirit; joy is the Spirit's deep reward; peace the mark of his presence; patience, kindness, goodness reveal a soul with resources beyond its own, resembling Christ;

81

faithfulness shows a heart held by the Spirit's strength; gentleness demonstrates a will that seeketh not its own; and self-control is what men call the inner unity that springs from being ruled from within by the Spirit of God. Then Paul adds a phrase which may clinch his argument 'the law was never meant for men like this!'; or perhaps he ends with irony 'surely the law does not forbid you to live like that!' The meaning, certainly, is plain: where the Spirit within a soul is bearing his gracious fruit, law is simply irrelevant.

In 5:25 the phrase is *live* by the Spirit, which recalls the panegyric in *Psalm* 1, comparing God's law to a great river continually refreshing, renewing, making fruitful the trees planted beside it. So the Spirit shall be a well, a spring, of life to those who live by. When to all this is added our waiting through the Spirit for the hope of righteousness (5:5), our reaping from the Spirit the harvest of eternal life (6:8), we realise how completely in Paul's thought the rule of the Holy Spirit in the Christian heart has taken the place of all that the law was intended to mean for the pious Jew.

The rule of the Spirit, then, is Paul's answer to the fears of the Judaist moralisers. One may attempt to bind men by regulations, frighten them with threats, dragoon them with commands, shame them with social censure; or one may seek to liberate them with ideas, transform them with kindled admiration, renew them with fresh motives, provoke them by challenging ideals, awaken new hopes in a new nature. The latter is the gospel's way to make man good *in freedom*, ruling him from within himself. Man's liberty finds its highest exercise in surrender to that regnant Spirit who disciplines the lower impulses (the 'desires of the Spirit' supplanting those of the flesh 5:17), and reproduces in him the likeness of Christ, for the Spirit *is* the Spirit of God's Son (4:6).

But what if these young Christians in Galatia do not possess the Spirit? Paul does not even contemplate the possibility. They being God's sons, 'God has sent the Spirit of his Son' into their hearts and Paul's (4:6); they had been 'born according to the Spirit', as in some extended sense Isaac had been (4:29); they had 'received the Spirit'—and not by the law (3:2); they had 'begun with the Spirit', God 'supplying' the Spirit to them (3:3, 5); this had proved the crowning 'blessing of Abraham' which they, though Gentiles, had come to inherit through Christ (3:14). Paul has no doubt that, being Christians, these readers of his possess the Spirit of Christ: and that answers all fears about the freedom they enjoy in Christ.

If, in spite of all this, we still feel that in *Galatians* Paul protests too much, it may be we should look a little deeper. Perhaps it was not only his jealousy for the Galatians' freedom, or his memory of Jewish bondage and frustration, that made him contend so strongly against those who would impose the safe reins of law upon dangerous liberty. Does not Paul's whole argument imply that the real purpose of spiritual freedom is precisely that we might remain flexible and responsive to the living Spirit of Christ? We tend to value freedom for its own sake, assuming that its value is obvious, never asking *why* men want it. The great pioneers of religious liberty knew why—they wanted to be free to obey Christ. They held themselves excused from obligations and loyalties that—in their view—conflicted with 'the crown rights of the Redeemer'. They contended for Christ as only Head and Lawgiver of church and conscience, and claimed liberty to be at the disposal of the Spirit.

Paul saw the same necessity. In a Judaist version of Christianity, something essential, and characteristic, and vital, would be lost. Bound to written codes, men would become deaf to living words of God; gazing on the past, they would miss the finger of God moving in the present; fettered to an ancient tradition, they would resist the Spirit as once the Jewish leaders had resisted and rejected Jesus—in the name of God and his law. Paul could never forget that tragic mistake. And he would not see it repeated among Christians. The temptation of the church has ever been to run away from spiritual liberty into organisation, orders, liturgy, creeds and regulations, to accredit the prophets, to affiliate the saints, to legislate the morals, to formularise the truth and label the faithful. Whereas the Spirit blows where it will, and they who are born of the Spirit must bend to his blowing. Paul's plea is just that—stand fast in your liberty, that the Spirit may have freedom among you.

This is not to minimise the dangers involved in spiritual freedom. Paul knows very well that 'he that sows to his own flesh will from the flesh reap corruption'; but he is equally confident that 'he who sows to the Spirit will from the Spirit reap eternal life' (6:8). To all the fearful questions which moralists and traditionalists, the conventional and the legalists, raise about the perils of too much freedom, Paul has one strong reply—The answer is the Spirit.

CHAPTER EIGHT

Emotional immaturity

It is strange that of all New Testament churches, the church at Corinth should be held up before modern Christians as worthy of emulation. Her reputation could hardly be worse; to be fair, neither could her situation.

The city's name was attended with slanderous epithets throughout the Graeco-Roman world; as a centre of idolatry, especially of idolatry coupled with debauchery, drunkenness, and gambling, Corinth was infamous. A melting-pot of races and cultures, the centre of a sea-going trade that gathered the riff-raff of the Mediterranean to her quaysides, and set on the fringe of the once-great Greek mainland so as to inherit Greek argumentativeness and loquacity without Greek intellect and love of truth, Corinth was a sorry birth-place for a Christian church. Yet here the gospel faced paganism *at its worst*, and won great victories. If it took time, patience, and discipline, to mature the first converts in Christian manners, faith, and stability, we can hardly be surprised. We certainly cannot throw stones.

The chief problems within the fellowship, as revealed in Paul's 'first' letter to the church, were those typical of emotional immaturity. Excitable, over-enthusiastic loyalty to rival parties and leaders led to what Paul deliberately describes as 'nursery-squabbling' among 'babes in Christ' (3:1–4). Men and women newly won from such paganism found the feelings harder to subdue to Christian purity than the mind to Christian truth, and Paul had to speak very sharply about immorality and fornication (5:1f; 6:12f). For the rest, an 'adolescent' problem of behaviour concerned ill-mannered attitudes at the Lord's Table, and a rowdy self-assertiveness in the services of worship, when order was sacrificed to fervour and mutual consideration to self-aggrandisement (11:17–14:40). It is no coincidence, but entirely typical of the New Testament, that the passages dealing with these main problems at Corinth are also those which expound most firmly the meaning, and the ministry, of the Holy Spirit in the church.

Rival leadership has been the bane of the church through all her centuries. It is natural that certain men and women should reveal gifts of speech, winsomeness, persuasiveness, compassion, greater than others can rise to: Christians are neither born equally endowed nor born again into uniformity. But great men cast long shadows, and whole movements, denominations and 'schools' are identified by individual names whose owners might not have approved such adulation. It is probable that Peter and Apollos would not approve the use of their names as party-cries at Corinth, but would, like Paul, condemn the damage done to fellowship. Beside rebuking the 'childishness' so revealed, Paul takes considerable trouble to expose the *falsity* of the whole situation.

Those who at Corinth insist 'I belong to Paul', 'I belong to Apollos', 'I belong to Cephas' (1:12) are *contradicting* the true nature of the church as the *one* body of Christ; the *one* field in which God alone gives the increase, whoever plants or waters; the *one* building which God alone indwells, and which the various workmen had better be careful how they build. If any leader so builds God's shrine, either with worthless materials, or in such fashion that the temple falls into fragments, 'him will God destroy. For God's temple is holy, and that temple you are', Christians assembled there in Corinth! (12:12; 3:5–17).

It is *by the Spirit* that God indwells the church, making it a shrine (3:16). It was by the Spirit that the separate and varied members came together to form one body: 'By one Spirit we were all baptised into one body—Jews or Greeks, slaves or free—and all were made to drink of one Spirit' (12:13). And it is by the Spirit, as Paul insists half-a-dozen times, 'by the *same* Spirit', that all the diverse gifts that enrich the church are bestowed, as he distributes to each member individually, as he wills (12:4–11). It is therefore a serious denial of experience and truth, to forget the oneness of the church, made one by the action of the one Spirit, indwelt, superintended, and endowed by the one Spirit, and divide over lesser loyalties to human leaders into mutually opposed fan clubs and parties that 'give the lie to' our unity in Christ. Here again, as in *Acts*, and as we shall find in *Ephesians*, the Spirit of Christ is emphatically *the Spirit of unity*: his action and power are never divisive.

Two difficult expressions used to underline this truth demand careful attention: 'baptised by one Spirit . . . made to drink of one Spirit' (12:13). The phrase 'baptised in [or with] the Spirit' seems to have begun with John the Baptist, as an appropriate parallel to 'baptised in [or with] water', marking the alternatives of purification by immersion in fires of judgement or purification by immersion in waters of repentance; and then to have been re-applied, in the light of Pentecost, to Christian experience of the Spirit, when Christian baptism (like Christ's baptism) came to be seen as a baptism of water and Spirit (*John* 3:5; see above, chapter 4, p. 40f). This seems a natural transference of the phrase, although Christians who make much of the gift of the Spirit are usually anxious to differentiate it entirely from water-baptism, and most of those who make much of water-baptism are equally anxious to deny that anything so meaningful as the gift of the Spirit happens in baptism! Most modern Christians, in any case, prefer a non-scriptural version of the phrase, namely 'the baptism *of* the Spirit', meaning presumably an experience granted by, or by the favour of, the Spirit. If however we prefer to adhere to New Testament language, we face this strange survival into a Christian epistle of sub-personal categories for the Spirit—as an element in which one may be immersed, or which one may drink. The Spirit as 'wind' in *John* 3, as 'poured out' in *Acts* 2, recall Old Testament usage: but it is Paul's habit to speak of the Spirit as fully personal, not least in his letters to Corinth: 'the Spirit who apportions as he will', 'the Spirit searches . . . taught by the Spirit', 'the Lord is the Spirit' (*1 Corinthians* 12:13; 2:10, 13; *2 Corinthians* 3:17). To speak of being 'immersed in', or of 'drinking' the Spirit seems to revert to impersonal ideas of the Spirit.

It is tempting to suppose a side-reference to drinking at the Eucharist, following the mention of baptism, but that explains nothing. Perhaps we must take refuge in the licence of metaphor. 'Baptised into Christ Jesus' (*Romans* 6:3; *Galatians* 3:27) has the same strange suggestion of 'immersion into a person' but, although 'baptised into Moses' (*1 Corinthians* 10:2) may give us pause, we do not usually find it difficult to speak of the Christian as henceforth 'in Christ', 'putting on Christ'. Christ becomes his 'element', his 'atmosphere', his 'world'. If the analogy is sound, then 'baptised in [or with] the Spirit' means initiated into an experience of the Spirit who thereby becomes—like the risen Christ—our 'element', our 'world'. 'To drink of one Spirit' presumably states the other side of this experience: just as the Christian is in Christ, though Christ is also in him, so the Christian lives 'in the Spirit' while the Spirit also indwells him. We may be sure that all this was clearer to the Corinthians, who knew Paul's impassioned speech and turns of phrase so much better than we do. But if Paul's language intrigues us, his meaning is plain: party divisions in the church are false to the unity into which the Spirit has brought us all.

Paul has something to say also about the originating cause of such schism. Though Peter's name is mentioned as one party-cry, the whole argument of chapters 1–4 is directed towards the Apollos party (as 4:6 declares). Apollos was 'an eloquent man, well versed in the scriptures, fervent in spirit', speaking and teaching 'accurately' and boldly the things concerning Jesus, and powerfully confuting the Jews in public (*Acts* 18:24–28). In contrast, Paul was 'unskilled in speaking', 'his bodily presence weak, his speech of no account', with none of the polish or persuasiveness of Greek wisdom or rhetoric to commend it (*2 Corinthians*

11:6; 10:10; *1 Corinthians* 2:4). Small wonder that when Apollos came on to Corinth, these eager, talkative, argumentative young Christians welcomed him with open ears. *This* was preaching! Here was someone to refute the critics, to win outsiders, to make the services exciting!

Paul offers no criticism of Apollos, but he warns sharply against the attempt to build faith upon the wisdom of the world, against relying upon the 'eloquent wisdom' which could empty the cross of its power; against 'the cleverness of the clever', 'the debater of this age', and the boast in human wisdom which knows not God, and which had no more sense than to crucify the Lord of glory. Far otherwise is the foundation of Christian faith. 'I decided to know nothing among you save Jesus Christ and him crucified. And I was with you in weakness and in much fear and trembling; and my speech and my message were not in plausible words of wisdom, but in demonstration of the Spirit and power, that your faith might not rest in the wisdom of men but in the power of God' (1:17–2:5).

We do speak wisdom, among those mature enough to grasp it! (2:6), for Christ is made unto us wisdom. But the fact is that the wisdom of God, the profound and eternal truths of our salvation, are not discoverable by human ingenuity: they are prepared for those who love God, and they are revealed through the Spirit, who searches everything, even the depths of God. As a man's own spirit searches a man's own thoughts, so 'no one comprehends the thoughts of God except the Spirit of God'. And 'we have received not the spirit of the world', its wisdom, rhetoric, argument, and intellectual pride, 'but the Spirit which is from

90

God, that we might understand the gifts bestowed on us by God' (2:10–12).

So, if our public speech is less than arresting, eloquent, compelling, by the world's standards, that cannot be helped. We impart God's truth, 'in words not taught by human wisdom but taught by the Spirit, interpreting spiritual truth in spiritual language' (or, less probably, 'to those who possess the Spirit', 2:13). To the unspiritual man, the gifts of the Spirit of God are 'folly', out of reach and beyond understanding, 'because they are spiritually discerned' (2:14). Faith stands upon spiritual insight, upon truth imparted by the Spirit to the spiritually inclined, not upon worldly wisdom and the ability to beat down opponents in debate. 'So let no one boast of men. All are yours . . . Paul, Apollos, Cephas . . . all are yours': enjoy them all, *but do not idolise anyone*: 'you are Christ's', not any leader's, and your faith stands in the demonstration of the Spirit and power, not in any man's *charisma* (3:21).

Here, as in John's presentation, the Spirit is the source of enlightenment and power, validating the gospel in the mind and experience of young converts, taking of the things of Christ and showing them to the teachable. Thus, to have the Spirit of God, in matters calling for careful judgement, is equivalent to possessing 'the mind of Christ' (7:40; 2:16); similar, again, is being given 'through the Spirit . . . the utterance of wisdom . . . the utterance of knowledge . . . faith, by the same Spirit' (12:8, 9). The 'intellectual' function of the Spirit, in his ministry towards believers, is everywhere in the New Testament. The Spirit of wisdom, revelation, understanding and conviction, is the answer to the over-valuation of particular teachers, however intellectually gifted, when their popularity splits the congregation into factions and spoils the fellowship of the church.

The reminder that the readers had once been 'immoral, idolaters, adulterers, homosexuals, thieves, greedy, drunkards, revilers . . .' but now have been 'washed . . . sanctified . . . justified in the name of the Lord Jesus Christ and in the Spirit of our God' (6:9, 11) carried a necessary warning to the immature at Corinth. They had been lifted so recently out of the sewer. Thoughts and habits clung about them that had no place in Christian life. One case within the church of 'a man living with his father's wife' shocked Paul into vigorous disciplinary action (5:1–5); almost incredibly, it seems that some who would hear the epistle read in the Christian assembly still needed to be warned against taking 'the members of Christ' and making them 'members of a prostitute' (6:15). But it was not simply a question of old habits dying hard, and old temptations refusing to be put down: there was argument at Corinth about this also. Some said, 'All things are lawful for me', justifying immorality as a demonstration of Christian freedom.

Against that perilous sophistry, Paul writes a brief but pungent paragraph (6:9f), reiterating that no immoral person will inherit the kingdom of God; recalling the convert's total break with the past— washing, sanctifying, being justified; insisting that though all things might be lawful, the Christian cannot consent to become again 'enslaved'. The body is not for immoral purposes, but for the Lord, who bought it with a price, who will raise it from death to glory, who has made our *bodies* members of his body:

how dare we then make them 'one flesh' with prostitutes! We are 'one spirit' with the Lord (6:17) and individually, separately, even physically, shrines of the Spirit, the *Holy* Spirit: 'Do you not know that your body is a temple of the Holy Spirit within you, which you have from God? . . . Glorify God in your body' (6:19, 20). The many individual shrines of the Spirit (6:19) make possible the indwelling of the Spirit within the total church, also, as a corporate temple (3:16).

For an immature Christian wrestling with sexual impurity, Paul's words are firm, clear in warning, instructive, sympathetic, reasonable, forthright, and above all, *bracing*. Here in a nutshell is the Christian ethic concerning sex and the body: our body is Christ's, by his purchase, and will be redeemed at last to glory; our body is a member of his body, to be reserved for his use and honour; our body, not our minds only but our physical body, is a shrine of the indwelling Spirit of holiness. *We are sacred persons: keep it that way*! Imagine the young Christian, hitherto sorely tried by the enticements around him, walking the squalid streets of Corinth with *that* thought uplifting his heart!

But the emotional immaturity of the newly-won church at Corinth was nowhere more in evidence than in disturbed services of worship. For their behaviour here, even Paul, ever ready to praise, could find no relieving morsel of approbation (11:17). At the Table, one remained hungry, another was drunken: Paul had to say 'it is not *the Lord*'s Supper that you eat' (11:20). In the public services also things often got out of hand: seemliness, order, were dispelled by fervent spontaneity (14:40); outsiders or unbelievers entering might well say the Christian worshippers were mad (14:23).

Apart from immaturity, the trouble lay in an embarrassment of spiritual gifts. Corinth 'came behind' no other church in the possession of grace-gifts (1:7); and 'gifts of the Spirit' (14:1) were highly prized and freely exercised. The variety of such gifts bestowed by the Spirit upon ordinary men and women in one local church is astonishing: the utterance of wisdom, the utterance of knowledge, faith, healing, working of miracles, prophecy, 'ability to distinguish between spirits', various kinds of tongues, the interpretation of tongues, the gifts necessary for apostles, teachers (probably the same as 'the utterance of knowledge'), helpers, administrators (12:4f, 28f). 'Distinguishing between spirits' probably relates to exorcism; the special gift of 'faith', distinct from 'working of miracles' apparently refers to the accomplishment of outstanding effects by daring, confidence, great vision or energy: 'faith which can remove mountains'. 'The utterance of wisdom' may be a gift for spiritual counselling. The function of prophecy is defined for us: 'he who prophesies speaks to men for their upbuilding and encouragement and consolation' (14:3). We may wish that the 'gift of various kinds of tongues' (12:10) had been explained as clearly.

At Pentecost, the apostles spoke under the power of the Spirit in languages already known to their hearers, though not—apparently—to themselves (*Acts* 2:6–8): no 'gift of interpretation' was involved. It has been argued that this is what 'tongues' means throughout the New Testament. So the relevant word is used some thirty times in the Greek Old Testament, and in *Acts*

2:6, the 'equivalent' word means a known variation of language, not unintelligible sounds. The 'translation' of tongues, the reference to 'kinds' or families of tongues (*1 Corinthians* 12:10; 14:27) as well as the parallel drawn with the *language* of Assyria (14:21), is all said to support this view, that 'tongues' means simply known, systematic languages of the world. But *are* they tongues 'of men', or 'of angels' (13:1)?

Nothing in the story of Cornelius (*Acts* 10:46) or of the disciples at Ephesus (*Acts* 19:6), defines the phenomenon, except that Peter saw the Cornelius event as equivalent to Pentecost ('the same gift' *Acts* 10:46, 47; 11:17). There is no hint that the tongues mentioned were 'unknown', for as the italics of the older version warn us, this word, *wherever* it occurs in connection with 'tongues' has been added by the translators (*1 Corinthians* 14:2, 4, 13, 14, 19, 27). It is remarkable too that in *Acts* and throughout *1 Corinthians* 14:2, 4, 13, 14, 19, the plural suggests 'languages', since 'unintelligible speech', or 'gibberish', has no plural (14:27 is the exception, referring to one individual with his 'hymn, lesson, revelation, tongue, or interpretation').

On the other hand, the need at Corinth for an interpreter to be present (14:27, 28), and the fact that interpretation itself is a gift of the Spirit (12:10) lends support to the usual view that the 'tongues' *at Corinth* (and we hear of them nowhere else, unless in *Acts* 19, if this was *not* the Pentecostal kind) were in fact unintelligible sounds uttered in spiritual ecstasy, when the soul enraptured by the Spirit expressed its joy in 'groanings which cannot be uttered'. Descriptions include 'a sort of croon, or musical lilt' (compare 14:7–8), or resembling madness (14:23), or barbarian tongues (14:21), even the language of angels (13:1). Reference to this phenomenon in the New Testament is confined to *1 Corinthians* 12–14 (? *Acts* 19); certainty is impossible, but the young soothsayer at Philippi (*Acts* 16) reminds us that such practices were known in paganism: the unintelligible 'voices' of the 'possessed' being interpreted as oracles, on payment of a fee, by the slave-masters. Apollo, Cassandra of Troy, the priestess of Delphi, the Sybil of Cumae, were famous 'oracles' whose utterances needed translation. Plutarch, Philo, and other ancient authors refer to 'ambiguous utterances, obscure sounds', 'religious frenzy', as marks of pagan spiritual ecstasy, when 'conscious reason was superseded in the highest reach of the soul in its quest for God.' The obscure fact mentioned in 12:3, that some professing to speak by the Spirit of God could call Jesus 'accursed', seems to indicate that a similar experience was possible among pagans, distinguishable from Christian inspiration only by the *content* of what was uttered. It could be that Christians at Corinth wished to show that in ecstasy, as in healings, their new faith came no whit behind their former religions.

However we decide to understand these 'glossolalia' at Corinth, it is important to notice that Paul's attitude to them is never wholly negative. 'I thank God that I speak in tongues more than you all' (14:18) can hardly be dismissed as an idle boast of facility in known languages; nor as a scornful 'I could do it, if I wanted such a thing!': such a thanksgiving must be taken as sincere. Any criticism Paul makes of tongues springs from sympathy. He would reserve tongues for private devotion and personal edification (14:2, 4), but will not forbid them in worship provided an interpreter is available (14:39, 28—the paragraph is about public worship; compare 14:5b). The practice, and the exuberant enthusiasm which it expressed, is neither attacked nor defended: it was evidence of vitality, at any rate, and of joy (14:5a).

But the practice is analysed and assessed. Tongues are placed last in each list of gifts of the Spirit (12: 4–10, 28–30), and not even mentioned in similar passages, as *Romans* 12:6f; *Ephesians* 4:11f. Tongues, Paul says, edify no one else (12:2–5), they issue no clear call to action (14:6f), they convert no one (14:23, 24 despite 22), and most devastating of Paul's assessments: 'In church, I would rather speak five words with my mind, in order to instruct others, than ten thousand words in a tongue' (14:19). 'Five–ten thousand' is a belittling estimate of value!

This is Paul's whole point: the comparative *value* of tongues, prophecy, and love. Prophecy is every way preferable, to be sought after, treasured. It was a gift widely possessed in the apostolic church (*Acts* 2:17; 11:27; 13:1; 15:32; 21:10; *1 Thessalonians* 5:20), and also imitated (*Matthew* 7:15; *1 John* 4:1); it is named first among gifts in *Romans* 12:6f, second to apostles in *1 Corinthians* 12:28 and *Ephesians* 4:11. In *1 Corinthians* 14 Paul argues at length that prophecy is a higher gift than tongues precisely because it edifies the Christian hearer, and also wins souls (14:1–6, 24). All the same, prophecy is to be heard with caution, 'weighed' (29): the church is not to be at the mercy of voluble enthusiasts. The prophets, too, must accept discipline, taking their turn one at a time, so that the worship-service is seemly, impressive, and orderly (14:29–33, 40).

But there is a more excellent way than either tongues,

prophecy, or any other of the gifts of the Spirit, that is the 'way', or 'fruit', of love. Without love, Paul boldly tells this highly endowed congregation, without *love*, tongues-speaking, whether with language of men or of angels; prophecy, however eloquent or enthusiastic; the Spirit's gift of knowledge, however useful; the energy of mountain-shifting faith; abounding generosity, even martyrdom—without love they are all worthless, empty, nothing, *futile* (12:31–13:3). And when prophecy, and tongues, and knowledge, and all other things we prize in immaturity, shall have passed away, or with coming manhood have been put away, love still will last, among the permanent things of Christianity—and, among them, the greatest (13:8–13).

Love, orderliness, and social value: such are the *criteria of assessment* for gifts which any man claims are of the Spirit, along with the primary requirement, the confession that Christ is Lord (12:3). The whole discussion is of the utmost importance, for the modern church as it was for Corinth. The abundance of spiritual gifts within that church, each gifted person clamouring for self-expression, made for great liveliness, exuberance, 'a living fellowship', and rowdiness. Paul will quench nothing, forbid nothing, condemn nothing: but he will plead, in the midst of the discussion, 'Brethren, do not be children in your thinking; be babes in evil, yes, but in thinking be mature' (14:20). And the sign of maturity, in this matter of the gifts of the Spirit, is a true understanding of the function of the Spirit in the church's life, and in consequence a *Christian* sense of what is important.

And Paul provides just that:
(i) The Spirit is sovereign in the giving of gifts: men may 'desire', even 'earnestly desire' them, and having

a gift may 'strive to excel' in building up the church—but nothing is said of striving to possess: the Spirit 'apportions to each one individually as he wills' (12:11, 31; 14:1, 12).

(ii) All the varied gifts are conferred by 'the same Spirit . . . the same Lord . . . the same God . . .' and so through the nine gifts, 'by one and the same Spirit' (12:4–11). No manifestation that proves to be divisive, therefore, can be from the Spirit of Christ, the Spirit of unity by whom 'we were all baptised into one body', the single source of the church's manifold endowments.

(iii) The gifts are for the benefit of all: 'to each is given the manifestation of the Spirit for the common good' (12:7)—*never* for self-aggrandisement, exhibition, or 'proof' of anything. That is why love is the essential accompaniment of the gifts, without which they are futile; and that is how the best gifts are to be recognised, as they do, or do not 'build up the church' (14:1–5).

(iv) No member can be so privileged or endowed as to imagine, or pretend, that he is independent of the rest. Neither can the delicate, beautiful, expressive, inexplicable *eye* say to the roughened, calloused, clumsy *hand*, nor the essential, mysterious *head* say to the humble, unlovely *foot*, 'I have no need of you'—and churches have all kinds of members! (12:14–26). The Spirit indwells and endows an interdependent, centrally governed, body of many closely inter-related members, not a charnel-house of severed limbs: and the supposed 'gift' that makes the individual proud and self-sufficient is not a gift of the Spirit.

(v) The Spirit is the source of the church's vitality, fervour, freshness, and power, her developing insight, and progress into truth; perhaps Paul would include praying, singing, praise and thanksgiving 'in the Spirit' (if a capital is correct, in that passage (14:15–17). The Spirit constantly equips the church for continuing ministry in a pagan world, so that unpromising individuals discover within themselves unsuspected capacities of speech, insight, leadership, action. But in what is sought after, admired, emphasised, honoured, and coveted within the church, Paul demands to see some value, something that expresses love, edifies others, glorifies Christ, transforms character, wins outsiders. That 'gifts' could be exciting, enjoyable, self-gratifying, was not in doubt, but Paul asks: Is it any use? If not, that hankering after the ecstatic and spectacular should be quickly outgrown, as among 'childish things'.

What we are permitted to see, in *1 Corinthians* especially though not only here, is the steady working out of Christian understanding of the Spirit to a second stage. The first stage finds illustration in *Luke* and *John*, as impersonal categories are replaced by the closest possible relation of the Spirit to Christ—the *personalisation* of men's thought about the Spirit. The second step draws the obvious, and essential, conclusion: that the Spirit who is 'the form of the contemporary Christ in the ongoing church' must, in all his manifestations, gifts and endowments, exhibit the character of Christ. This is Paul's version of 'test the spirits' (compare *1 John* 4:1). His wholly sympathetic, yet relentless, *moralisation* of Christian understanding of the Spirit spelled the overthrow of the merely spectacular, and the establishment of the Christlike, as the sign of the presence of the Spirit in the individual and the church.

The evidence of the Spirit's power is no longer a sensual and violent guerrilla tearing lions to pieces and laying about him with the jawbone of an ass (*Judges* 14:6; 15:14f); nor an individual so beside himself with ungovernable emotion that he can shout with glee 'Jesus is accursed' (12:3); nor yet an assembly of worshippers so unruly and unintelligible that the occasional visitor concludes they are demented (14:23). From time to time the hunger for a more immediate experience of God, for spiritual joy, for a sense of power, for 'utter and uninhibited dedication' for some assurance of the spiritual world, and sometimes, sheer impatience with the deadliness of Christian institutions lacking Christian life, has led eager people to 'return to Corinth' movements. Sometimes the results include eccentric emotional manifestations, bizarre behaviour, and even (more than once in history) immorality, community of wives, 'love-ins' and the like. People are 'slain by the Spirit' into unconsciousness or paralysis; catalepsy, spasmodic jerking, hallucinations, visions of angels, compulsive nudity, pet dogs 'speaking with tongues'—there is no limit to the phenomena claimed to be manifestations of the Spirit. The only Christian reaction is that of Paul: whatever is truly of the Spirit of Christ will acknowledge his lordship, and be morally and socially worthy of Christ.

It is not at all surprising that converts with a background like that of Corinth have a long way to climb and need a fair time to grow: only those who have shared the daunting struggle can truly sympathise. But the gospel is the power of God unto salvation, and Christ is able to save to the uttermost, while for the natural difficulties of spiritual 'adolescence' there is provision. When immature enthusiasms are overcharged with merely individual loyalties, the Spirit of unity binds all in one; when immature awakening is too impressed with merely human wisdom, the Spirit of truth will lead to deeper understanding; when immature sensuality threatens the soul, the Spirit of purity will indwell and sanctify; when immature exuberance over-values the emotional elements in worship, the Spirit who bestows all gifts will discipline to the common good. In fact, to all the problems of Christian immaturity, the answer is the Spirit.

CHAPTER NINE

The diverse community

'Paul's masterpiece, the very crown of the epistles';
'the most modern of the New Testament writings': so
Ephesians has been described, and on both counts we
would expect the letter to say much about the Spirit.
And so it does, but once again the Spirit is not the
main subject. He is referred to secondarily, in support
of a theme and purpose which lie elsewhere.

Some incidental allusions show how often the Spirit
recurs to Paul's mind. The prayer that God might give
to the Ephesians 'a' spirit of wisdom and of revelation
(1:17) could request simply 'a wise human spirit'
(compare 'spiritual wisdom and understanding'
Colossians 1:9, and 'the spirit of your minds' *Ephesians*
4:23); but in 3:5 the knowledge of the mystery of
Christ is given 'by the Spirit', and there is no doubt
that Paul (like John) would trace all Christian
wisdom and enlightenment to the Spirit of truth. In
the same way, 4:3 could mean simply 'spiritual unity',
but the next verse refers to the Spirit in the same connection, so Paul probably means 'the unity which the
Spirit bestows'. In 3:16–20, being 'strengthened with
might through his Spirit in the inner man', Christ
dwelling in our hearts through faith, and 'the power at
work within us' are closely linked. Such phrases
illustrate how automatically, whenever Paul considers

the resources for Christian living, he thinks at once of the Spirit of wisdom, of power, and of Christ.

In three different schools of New Testament thought, the word of God is likened to a sword (6:17; *Hebrews* 4:12; *Revelation* 1:16; 2:16; 19:15). God's truth certainly cuts its way to the heart of man, and wins God's battles. But 'the sword *of the Spirit*' is a surprising phrase. Nowhere else do we meet the Spirit armed, conducting warfare, or associated with military language. Nor is it very clear how the sword of the Spirit comes to be in the hand of the Christian. The rest of the Christian's armour consists of spiritual qualities, truth, righteousness, peaceableness, faith, an experience of salvation: why not this item also? In *2 Corinthians* 10 Paul disparages worldly warfare with carnal weapons in favour of spiritual warfare with reasonable argument and 'thoughts taken captive'. It seems probable that that is Paul's meaning in *Ephesians* too: 'take the only weapon appropriate to spiritual warfare, a spiritual sword, namely the word of God.'

At 5:9; Paul wrote, not 'the fruit of the Spirit' but 'the fruit of light'. None of the passing allusions tells us anything new about the Christian experience of the Spirit: for what is, in some degree, distinctive in *Ephesians* we must consider the practical question which evoked this epistle, and discover how the Spirit comes into Paul's prescription for dealing with it. Of the dominant theme of this apostolic circular there can be no doubt: Paul is writing of 'the mystery of God's will' (1:9), what God is after in Christ. This is mentioned in 1:5, and echoes through the first chapters in words like choice, destiny, predestination, 'what is decreed in the design of him who carries out everything according to the counsel of his own will'; that to which we are called, the secret disclosed, the plan of the mystery, the eternal purpose. Such is Paul's great subject—what God is doing.

And he defines it equally clearly: 'He has made known to us in all wisdom and insight the mystery of his will, according to his purpose which he set forth in Christ as a plan for the fullness of time, to unite all things in him, things in heaven and things on earth.' '*To unite*' is a most interesting expression, in Greek: it contains the word 'head', the idea of 'bringing things to a head', strictly, of 'bringing things under one head', 'recapitulating', 'summing up'. When Greek schoolboys did their arithmetic, adding *up* a column of figures, they wrote the total at the top, not at the bottom. The process of addition was, in fact, 'bringing to a head', 'summing *up*'. So the word came to mean, also, the summing up of the chief points in an argument, at the end of a speech, the recapitulation— gathering the scattered threads of discussion and tying them into a knot, as well as gathering together the different amounts and making them a total. So Moffatt translates God's purpose: 'to gather up all things in Christ'.

God is working to bring all things under Christ's headship, to establish in him a focus, a point of unity, in which to unite the universe. And the prefix to the Greek word probably means 'doing it again'—after it has once been done, and undone; all things are to be gathered up *again*, reunited, in Christ. *God is faced with a fragmented universe.* Man is at odds with God, at odds with man, at odds with himself. Disruptive forces have destroyed the primeval harmony; a random, self-assertive factor has entered the total scheme of things. The modern picture of the physical universe, of an infinity of bits, stars, planets, galaxies, nebulae, all flying outward from each other in an expanding immensity of space, each particle thrusting to get farther and farther from its fellow, is very like the New Testament picture of our world. Co-existence, cohesion, co-operation, merely holding society together, requires supreme effort and great patience. Disintegration, independence, revolt, are watchwords natural to man; within human nature is no centre of gravity drawing the elements of the cosmos together, only competitive belligerence, each struggling for existence against his fellow.

Sad experience warning him of the peril involved, man fosters his private friendships, societies, clubs, domestic circles, patriotism, racial unities, and sometimes totalitarian unity imposed by force: but every point of unity so set up, and every circle of fellowship so defined, proves to be also exclusive, breaking away from some larger whole. Nor is this all. There is yet deeper incoherence in the heart of things, in the endless conflict of right and wrong, spirit and flesh, mechanism and freedom, the law of the physical world and the liberty of the human spirit. Man's spiritual aspiration seems to be a stranger in a predetermined universe, and all his advancing knowledge appears to deny his conscience, his own worth, and his responsibility. While if man looks within himself, he finds a conflict of instinct with reason, of something 'a little lower than the angels' against something barely higher than the brutes, a veneer of civilised education that scarcely restrains potentialities of bitterness, prejudice, falsehood, pride, cruelty, lust and hate that could so easily tear him in pieces.

In Christ God sets himself to reduce to order the universal chaos, to re-establish the original coherence, to subdue all things afresh under one head. Christ is set forth as the point of reconciliation, the principle and the moving power of integration, the focus of the diverse forces, the inner unity of the world. 'He was before all things, and in him all things hold together' Paul told the Colossians; 'through him God was pleased to reconcile to himself all things, whether on earth or in heaven, making peace by the blood of his cross.' John declared that Jesus should die to gather together in one all the children of God scattered abroad (*John* 11:52); the *Book of Revelation* records the testimony: 'Thou wast slain and by thy blood didst ransom men for God from every tribe and tongue and people and nation . . .'—uniting natural, cultural, racial and political divisions at once (*Revelation* 5:9). 'I, if I be lifted up,' said Jesus, 'will draw all men unto me' (*John* 12:32).

Paul saw the disruption of the universe extended to 'principalities and powers in heavenly places': the source of universal disharmony lay in the invisible world, among the world-rulers of this darkness, the spiritual hosts of wickedness in the eternal sphere. The originating cause was superhuman, the forces behind it demonic; reconciliation in Christ must therefore include 'things in heaven' as well as 'things on earth'. With, or if necessary without, their consent, *all things* must be subjected again to Christ. The unity God is pursuing is thus a transcendental reintegration of the whole created universe, the reduction to peace and calm not only of the turbulent sea of Galilee (a symbol-miracle), not only of the seething discord in human hearts, not only of the warring elements within society, and the bitter strife which rends his world-wide family, but beyond and including all this, of the cosmic forces of disruption and rebellion whence all lesser discords flow.

The first step towards that unity has already been taken: for God has recruited from among the rebellious and disobedient those who have responded to his call. He has united them with Christ, made them alive *together*, raised them up *together*, made them sit *together*, in Christ, above the warring elements in the heavenly places. Such now are united within themselves, united with each other, united with Christ, and lifted above the discord. So has emerged the church, the reunifying purpose of God *made visible*. Out of the sharpest, deepest, bitterest discord of all in human society has risen a unity, a fellowship, undreamt of—the church of Christ across the world, created, united and reconciled, in Christ.

Among the 'Ephesian' congregations were those who had been Gentiles, in Jewish eyes the pagan, the heathen; the uncircumcised—a term of contempt; those with no share in the messianic hope—outsiders; aliens to the spiritual commonwealth of God's people; strangers to the ancient promises made to Israel; hopeless ones, godless ones, men and women 'far off' in far countries of the soul; the other side of every dividing wall—foreigners without hope—*Paul exhausts the vocabulary of division and alienation in describing what his readers had been* (2:11–19). This is the social expression of the fragmented universe, religious, social, patriotic, racial bitterness holding human hearts apart. Such they were: but now, having come to be in Christ, who is peace and makes peace, those far away are brought near, the barriers are down, the feud is ended. All are reconciled; strangers, foreigners, godless no longer, they form one household of God, fellow-citizens in the city of God, a superstructure reared on one foundation-stone, a temple for the habitation of God.

Here is the church, in five metaphors: a city or commonwealth, politically unified; a household of God, domestically unified; a structure God is building through history, foundationally unified; a temple unified by consecration to one purpose; a habitation unified through all lands and all generations by the indwelling of one Spirit. God's reconciling purpose has already borne fruit, for this is fact not dream, or doctrine. The stone, Christ, has dropped into the restless pool of humanity, and the mastering ripples have spread outwards to encircle Jew and Gentile, rich and poor, barbarian, Scythian, bond, free, male, female, old and young. Here is the church united by the sevenfold cord—one body, one Spirit, one hope for which they are called, one Lord, one faith, one baptism, one God and Father of all, who is over all, through all, and in all (4:4–6). Even the powers in heavenly places must see it happening, and realise through the church the manifold wisdom, and the victory, of God (3:10). So must we realise it, grasping with all the saints the length, breadth, height and depth of the surpassing love of God, who has thus taken us from rebellion and conflict to make us one in Christ's peace (3:18–19). The ongoing purpose of God, to reduce the chaos of the world to order and re-establish the original coherence of things, is made visible among the facts of history, and has found its vehicle and instrument, in the church of the already reconciled.

That is all very well. The sweep of Paul's vision of the church is exhilarating, his emphasis upon what was already accomplished is reassuring: but we all know there is more to be said. The church that history has known, the church we see around us still, hardly deserves Paul's thrilling metaphors, scarcely provides any evidence of the sevenfold bond. We must penetrate far beneath appearances, must see the church transfigured by the purposes of God, must exercise a courageous faith, to recognise in the muddle and diversity of ecclesiastical institutions the church that Paul describes. But that is exactly Paul's pastoral purpose also, in writing *Ephesians*, to call the Asian churches to exercise that penetrating insight, vision, and courageous faith, and see themselves amidst all *their* diversity and inadequacies as the church through which the unification of the world would yet be achieved.

For they *were* diverse. That exhaustive list of alienations overcome in Christ is itself the evidence of their varied backgrounds. If the emphasis falls on the division of Jew and Gentile, with the mention of circumcision, the commonwealth of Israel, the covenants, the law of commandments like a dividing wall, that is not only because a Jew is writing, but because the racial-religious division was the deepest and most intractable in the ancient world. It would be hard to say on which side lay the staunchest pride, or the deepest contempt for the other: and every powerful influence in human life, religion, patriotism, history, culture, and blood, kept Jew and Gentile apart. Even in the modern world nothing more irrevocably divides men than did that mutual hostility of Gentile and Jew: only in the Christian church did the two ever meet in amity, in what Paul actually calls 'one new man in place of the two' (2:15), a new sort of humanity, neither Jewish nor Gentile but Christian.

• Among the Jews themselves, of course, some were strict, some lax, some Hellenist in outlook, some orthodox, some ascetic like the Essenes. Almost every reference Paul makes to the Gentiles' former days suggests they too had varied backgrounds. They had been 'trespassers', following the course of this world, passionate, sensual, 'children of wrath', their lives marked by futility, darkened understanding, ignorance, callousness, greed and licentiousness: a repeated word is 'disobedience', and another revealing term twice used is 'alienated'. The life from which they had come had evidently been anything but orderly, placid, disciplined, conforming to social ideals. Nor, even now, within the church, are all the members alike: for a variety of ministries, of apostles, prophets, teachers, evangelists, cater for different needs, equipped by the same ascending Lord to enable all to grow in the unity of the faith to the measure of the stature of the fullness of Christ. The variety of the church, and of its ministry, is not as moderns persuade themselves a contradiction of the church's unity, but (Paul says) a contribution to it.

The members of the Asian churches were certainly diverse: they were also divisive. Paul was far too much a realist to imagine that all the converts in the local churches had conquered overnight the divisive and anti-social tendencies of their earlier lives. His appeal is precisely that they shall learn the *unifying* virtues, the reconciling, cohesive qualities of the mature Christian character: 'with all lowliness and meekness, with patience, forbearing one another in love, eager to maintain the unity of the Spirit in the bond of peace' (4:2, 3). Hence the call to leave resolutely behind the old divisive, antagonistic ways, and to 'walk worthy' of their special calling to be agents of the divine purpose of reconciliation. They must leave behind all childish fickleness of mind, too easily persuaded, unreliable (4:14); they must set aside every attitude, prejudice, habit of mind and of emotion, that would disrupt the instrument upon which God relies to fulfil his unifying purpose.

This is the only acceptable explanation of those surprising, and disturbing, imperatives in 4:25–5:4. The church members must put away lies, and learn to speak the truth only. One would have hoped that Christians needed no such counsel: but the reason given is significant, 'we are members one of another'. Lying is a breach of fellowship; it destroys mutual trust; it creates separation, and disruption, violating the unity to serve which we are called. The church member must put a curb upon his anger, tempering its strength and limiting its duration, giving 'no opportunity to the devil' to get in among Christians divisively. The church member must not steal, becoming needlessly dependent on the common resources; he must instead contribute towards them, working diligently at honest tasks so as to give to the common pool. Again the reason offered is significant: it is the social obligation of honest work that is emphasised.

The church member must take care about his conversation, avoiding slander, criticism, and all else that destroys fellowship, using his tongue only for edification and graciousness, avoiding everything repellent (literally 'rotten') that would drive people from each other. And the church member must abandon the competitive, rival, ambitious, get-ahead-and-let-others-look-after-themselves reaction to life, replacing 'all bitterness, wrath, anger, clamour, slander and malice' with kindness, tenderness, readiness to forgive, and a social attitude of loving and fragrant self-sacrifice, 'imitating God'. All the duties inculcated in this condensed and penetrating passage are obvious, even elementary: their reasons, and their context, reveal them to be factors in a process of 'socialisation', by which discordant, abrasive individualism, alienated and indrawn, is moulded to the cohesive, outgoing, co-operating, tractable and reconcilable personality, in which the grace of God that is in courtesy, and the love of Christ that is in Christian comradeship, govern every word and act and attitude.

Very plainly, therefore, Paul does not imagine that the far-reaching purpose of God is near completion in the churches to which he writes. His hope is to move a diverse and divisive Christian community nearer to the purpose of their calling in Christ: 'I therefore, a prisoner for the Lord, beg you to lead a life worthy of the calling to which you have been called', namely, to be servants of him who seeks to 'unite all things in Christ'. To persuade them to fulfil that reconciling vocation, Paul reminds them what the purpose is, invites them to look at what has already been accomplished, appeals to them to leave the past behind, and *remember the presence among them of the Holy Spirit of God.*

  That is where the Spirit enters the great argument of *Ephesians.* The Spirit of community, of fellowship, already met in *Acts*, the Spirit of unity portrayed in *1 Corinthians*, the Spirit linked in scattered references with love and fellowship, is here presented on a far wider canvas, against the background of the timeless divine purpose to make all things one in Christ, as the Spirit of universal reconciliation. It is for this reason, probably, that *Ephesians* is felt to be 'modern' in tone and in message. For the unity of the church, and the unity of mankind, are essentially modern preoccupations: and both are here related directly to the Spirit who makes all things one in Christ.

Of all the splendid things said in this epistle about the church, none is more breathtaking than the description, 'the whole structure . . . a holy temple in the Lord; in whom you also are built into it for a dwelling place of God in the Spirit' (2:21, 22). According to John's gospel, after Jesus had 'cleansed' the Temple in Jerusalem, he spoke of its destruction and rebuilding 'in three days', which John carefully explained as referring to his body, in some sense replacing the Temple as the centre of worship. Later Jesus told a woman in Samaria that the time was coming when neither at her building, nor at that in Jerusalem, would men worship, but 'in spirit and in truth'; and Stephen likewise challenged the age-old tradition that 'localised' God in 'houses made with hands'. Paul had declared to the Corinthians that they constituted the temple of the Spirit, both as individuals and as a corporate assembly (*1 Corinthians* 6:19; 3:16, 17). Peter, too, makes much of the living stones built into a spiritual house for priesthood and sacrifice acceptable to God (*1 Peter* 2:5). It is not exaggeration, therefore, to find here in *Ephesians* a theme of early Christian wonder: that God is raising through history a growing Temple fashioned from living souls, in which he might dwell among men, far more closely, more gloriously than ever in earthly shrine, by the presence and power of his living Spirit in the hearts of men.

Within the living church of the redeemed, in successive generations, God tabernacles among men. The church is the divine society: by her the Spirit speaks, through her he acts, in her he dwells, by her he witnesses to Christ, and, so long as the church endures, God's Spirit has not ceased to strive with men. Fallible, diverse, scattered, often oppressed, the divine society remains the habitation of God, and remains, despite all appearances, *one*. There can no more be many churches than there are many Holy Spirits: that is why Paul insists 'there is one body, and one Spirit' and charges members to maintain the unity not merely of a common faith, mind, outlook, experience, but the 'unity of the Spirit', the single life, the living 'soul', of the body of Christ on earth.

The 'stones' comprising this human shrine of the reconciling Spirit are themselves the fruit of the process of reconciliation. Each has been drawn, by the gospel, out of his isolation, his inner aloneness, his hostility towards God and antagonism towards men, into a salvation-experience which links him in the living fellowship of Christ and the church. At the heart of his reconciliation to God, to others, to himself and to life, lies acceptance with God: and the crucial expression of that acceptance is the experience of entrance, unrejected and unafraid, into the immediate presence of God. 'Through Christ we both' [that is, Jew and Gentile] 'have access in one Spirit to the Father' (2:18). Paul says this with all the awe and surprise of a Jew who through childhood and youth and into manhood had been taught that God is unapproachable, that curtains covered the Holy of Holies, to intrude beyond which meant death. Now, the Father welcomes, Christ opens up the way, and the Spirit draws the worshipper into the Presence: 'since we are justified by faith, we have peace with God through our Lord Jesus Christ. Through him we have obtained access to this grace in which we stand . . .' (*Romans* 5:1, 2). The diverse membership is bound in one by sharing together in the highest of all privileges and the deepest of all joys: the reconciling church is the church of the reconciled, testifying out of personal and continuing experience how the Spirit, through Christ, has brought those once far off very nigh indeed to God the Father.

Those so brought near by the Spirit are also sealed by him as members of the divine society (1:13; 4:30). In *2 Corinthians* 1:22 the sealing appears to be additional to the gift of the Spirit, seal and Spirit being 'a guarantee' (so *2 Corinthians* 5:5). In *Ephesians*, seal and Spirit are identified, and constitute 'the guarantee of our inheritance until we acquire possession of it'; 'we are sealed for the day of redemption'. The familiar sealing for authentication of documents (*Revelation* 5:1) seems a less likely analogy than the sealing of goods, cargoes, cattle and slaves, already purchased but awaiting collection, or redemption, in due course. One implication, 'sealed for safe keeping' (*Revelation* 7:2f), makes the individuals so privileged members of a people, an elect group, exempt from the general distress. A slight confirmation of this corporate aspect of sealing arises from the link of *seal* with *inheritance* and *redemption*: for 'inheritance' has all the sacred

116

associations of Israel's ancient covenant of a land and a people for God, and the promises made to the people whom God possessed; 'redemption', likewise, was no merely individual experience. The main significance of this sealing by the Spirit is however beyond doubt: possession of the Spirit is an interim mark of divine ownership, shared by all God's people, and assumed therefore to be upon all who are the Lord's. Not to have the Spirit is (again) not to be his.

There is no surer guarantee than a first instalment, a foretaste, a down-payment that pledges further instalments in kind. Such is the literal meaning of the 'guarantee' given under the Spirit's seal. In prosaic and practical terms, what is indicated is an experience enjoyed already which points forward to 'more of the same', namely present enjoyment of life within the Spirit-indwelt community. Startlingly, the one parallel experience that springs to Paul's mind is intoxication: 'Be not drunk with wine but be filled with the Spirit' (5:18), which curiously echoes Peter's explanation on the day of Pentecost, that the disciples were not 'drunken as you suppose'. A mood, an emotional tone, stimulating, joyous, relaxing, with a suggestion of sheer abandonment to a glorious time and a glow of soul, is surely implied. Not to press the point too hard, Paul immediately adds that the joy is *shared*, as Christian believers in social assembly address to each other psalms, hymns, spiritual songs, singing and making melody from the heart, and always and for everything giving thanks, a grateful hallelujah! Joy may be individually kindled, but it is contagious, and life in the Spirit, likewise, is infectious in its exuberance and deep happiness. Prayer in the Spirit, too, is both a private exercise and a shared supplication 'for all saints', as we pray with the Spirit who also makes intercession for us (6:18).

In such Spirit-filled hours we taste beforehand the 'earnest' and pledge of our inheritance, eternal life. Unfortunately, though this is the nature and the norm of life in the Spirit-filled fellowship, it is not our invariable experience. Circumstances can arise in which the *felt* presence of the Spirit may be at a minimum, through unbelief, or unresponsiveness, through carelessness of conduct, uncleanness of mind, strife between members. The Spirit's power, enlightenment, encouragement, and joy seem to recede, to be scarcely discernible. This is the effect, says Paul, especially of those anti-social attitudes proscribed in 4:25–31, untruthfulness, dishonesty, unclean and frivolous talk, and the rest. Since the fellowship into which the convert comes is a corporate incarnation of the Holy Spirit, he must learn to behave as always in the presence of the Spirit; he must do, say, think, nothing to vex or 'grieve' the Spirit dwelling within the group (4:30).

This obligation would be more dramatically felt in a church assembly where at any moment someone might break into 'tongues' or prophecy, or lay hands upon an epileptic and heal him. But the lack of a dramatic *sense* of obligation does not affect its truth: if we believe that the Spirit indwells the Christian fellowship, then whatever injures fellowship grieves the Spirit. We know by sad experince how true this is. When gossip, anger, foolish talk, slander, argument, introduce division, 'the spiritual temperature' of the fellowship declines, the power wanes, insight becomes confused, and we realise that the Spirit within the group has been 'grieved'—so far as his conscious presence is concerned, we feel he has 'withdrawn'. Regrettably, although the indwelling of the Spirit within the church is a corporate experience, the grieving of the Spirit is all too often the act of wilful, selfish, insensitive individuals.

The distinctive message of *Ephesians*, that in seeking to reduce the universe to one in Christ God has set the church within society to be the shrine of the all-reconciling Spirit, moves to the centre of Christian thought about the Spirit his *corporate* presence and function within the divine society. When the church herself is mixed in race and background, and even more so in modern days than in the cosier world of the Mediterranean empire; when she is divided also internally by differences of national culture, sectarian loyalty, historical circumstance, theological emphasis, and (strangest of all) by disagreements about the reconciling Spirit, the evidence of the Spirit's presence and power dwindle and almost disappear. How to reshape her worship, her organisation, her government, her methods, her approach to men, to give maximum freedom to the Spirit within her, are among the contemporary church's major problems. But with *Ephesians* in our hands, there can be no question that to these, and every other problem of the divine but diverse and divided community, the answer is the Spirit.

CHAPTER TEN

Spiritual confusion

John's 'perfect gem' of an epistle has just one hundred and five verses, yet John manages to say 'we know' or 'you know' or 'we are sure' about thirty-five times, and to mention belief, testimony, confidence, teaching, confessing, deceiving and the like at least thirty times. Something, obviously, needs to be clarified: eight times he insists '*By this* we know . . .'

Confusion has arisen through the defection of trusted Christian leaders who have left the apostolic churches to found rival groups, taking fellow-Christians with them and gathering a considerable following among enquirers who might otherwise have joined the apostolic circle (2:18, 19; 4:5). John pleads with the remainder to stay in their original faith and fellowship (2:24; 1:3). On the general principle that what John strenuously argues *for* his opponents must have been calling in question, we learn that the immediate occasion of this rift among believers was some philosophic-sounding reinterpretation of the gospel which rejected the incarnation of Christ, probably holding that the material body was incurably evil (John returns to this theme twenty-three times); the schismatics rejected also the Christian teaching upon morality, for John supplies fifteen reasons in eight verses why the Christian must not tolerate sin

(3:3–10). Similarly, there was evidently some argument that commandments do not concern mature Christian men, for John argues this point fourteen times, affirming especially the 'new commandment' of love.

It might appear that such direct contradiction of essential Christian doctrine and ethics would be only too clearly anti-Christian, as John calls it (2:18, 22; 4:3). But the rival leaders claimed to be only 'advanced' and 'perfect' Christians (*2 John* 9), with greater understanding of the gospel, a surer experience of God, and a more secure status 'beyond good and evil'. They claimed not to have sinned, and so to need no forgiveness; and to have no sin, and so to need no warning against it (1:8–10). They boasted of 'knowing God', being born again, walking in the light, having fellowship with God, 'abiding in Christ', being inspired, loving God, being 'in God' and 'of God', having the Spirit, possessing the gift of prophecy. These were precisely the levels of spiritual experience deeply desired by orthodox believers, loyal to 'that which was from the beginning'. How then could heretical teachers claim to have attained all this? Who could tell if the claims were true? Who was in the right, and how do we know?

John considers how we may distinguish truth from falsehood, genuine Christian experience from imitative mockery, some seventeen times, offering various criteria of truth by which we may know we have eternal life (5:13 for example). The letter has been called 'The Tests of Life', and it offers a searching check-list for self-examination. Its climax is the threefold reaffirmation, '*We know* that any one born of God does not sin . . . *We know* that we are of God . . . *We know* that the Son of God has come and has

given us understanding . . . and we are in him . . .
This is the true God and eternal life . . .' Among these
criteria for testing religious claims John sets walking
in the light, abhorring sin, loving our brother, holding
fast the original confession of Christ, growing in
Christ-likeness, But along with these—*not separately
from them* but probably as their source—John
includes the Christian experience of the Spirit:

> By this we know that he abides in us, by the Spirit
> which he has given us (3:24);
> By this we know that we abide in him and he in us,
> because he has given us of his own Spirit (4:13);
> The anointing which you received from him abides
> in you, and you have no need that any one should
> teach you . . . his anointing teaches you about
> everything, and is true (2:27);
> The Spirit is the witness, because the Spirit is the
> truth (5:7);
> There are three witnesses, the Spirit . . . (5:8).

There are of course two main difficulties in appeal-
ing to the experience of the Spirit as evidence of genuine
Christian life. One is that every teacher, however
heretical, and everyone who professes religion, however misled, claims to be inspired: in the Christian
tradition, to be speaking by the Spirit. The other
difficulty is that the appeal to the Spirit appears
entirely subjective, a matter of inward feelings,
motions, impressions, unprovable, and safe from any
searching test.

With the first difficulty, John deals quite summarily.
Of course there are many kinds of inspiration: 'Test
the spirits!' Try for identification by origin! Jesus had

warned of false prophets; and Paul mentioned some who apparently claimed to speak by the Spirit of Jesus when they called Jesus accursed, and he demanded acknowledgement of the lordship of Christ as proof that the inspiration claimed was truly of God. An early Christian handbook of instruction warns that 'not everyone who speaks in a spirit is a prophet; he is only a prophet if he walks in the ways of the Lord' (*Didache* 11:8). John's test for 'every so-called spirit', every claimed source of inspiration, is 'What does it say?' If it confesses that Jesus Christ is come in the flesh, a true and literal incarnation of the divine Christ made flesh for us, then the inspiration behind it is 'of God'. 'By this you know the Spirit of God . . . By this we know the spirit of truth and the spirit of error' (4:1–6).

The difference from Paul's test is not great—nor yet from that of the *Didache*: the touchstone revealing the true gold of Christian experience is the confession of Christ as Lord, as ruler of one's ways, as truly God and truly man. John makes no allowance for thoughtless, impulsive, or merely nominal confession of Christ; the cost of such a confession was too severe, in loss of family, disinheritance, exclusion from the synagogue, fine, imprisonment, even death. Empty profession was as yet very rare, Moreover, such confession was made in public; such acknowledgement of Christ as Lord and Son of God was the crucial point at which a convert entered the church through baptism and took his place with the people of God before the world. As Paul said, no man could take that fateful step but by the Holy Spirit: so John here represents the Spirit as the inspirer of the true confession of Jesus as the Christ. In consequence, such confession is one sure criterion of his presence in a life. Often, that first confession of Christ is associated with other objective 'signs', like 'tongues-speaking', or manifest gladness of heart; later the evident change of direction in the convert's whole personality, his growing obedience, zeal, righteousness, and Christ-like love, were equally objective signs, and criteria, of the Spirit within a soul. The appeal therefore is not to subjective feelings, but to the *evidence* of the Spirit in true public confession and a manifold change of character: by these we recognise the source of inspiration to be the Spirit of Christ.

In dealing with the first difficulty, the source of inspiration, John has also dealt in part with the second, the subjectivity of the test: but he adds a further point, loyalty to those whom in our hearts we *know* to be people of God. The spirit of anti-Christ finds ready hearing 'in the world'; those who speak by such inspiration 'are of the world, therefore what they say is of the world, and the world listens to them'. That is some indication of the source of their inspiration. 'We' on the other hand (the 'we' of the apostolic fellowship) 'are of God. Whoever knows God listens to us, and he who is not of God does not listen to us. By this we know the spirit of truth and the spirit of error.' The argument strikes us as self-confident, but John strives to throw around it an appeal to the judgement of one's best, most trusted, friends. In this confusion as to what is truth and where real inspiration lies, it is sound counsel to consider the *sort* of people among whom secession throws us.

The bewildered convert, distrustful of his own wisdom, seeking honestly the word of Christ among conflicting voices, at least knows the quality of those among whom he came to know the Lord. It is safe advice, at least as a start, to cling to those whom you have learned to trust, admire, and love for Christ's sake. If those already known to be 'of God' are cautious, unconvinced, waiting to see where God's truth lies, then it will be wise to look outside oneself and take refuge for a time in others' judgement, and wait for light. The worldly 'success' of new teachers is nothing compared with the spiritual quality of those who have hitherto led us into blessing. We shall come to realise, as we mature, that the very independence of mind by which we assess the world's ways, and choose the truth with God's few rather than the smart slogans of the latest cult, is strong evidence of the ministry of the Spirit towards us. We are learning thereby that he that is in us is greater than he that is in the world (4:4): and by that inner freedom and victory over worldliness we recognise once more the presence of the Spirit.

As public confession of Christ, changed character, and steadfast allegiance to the godly, are objective evidence of the Spirit's work within us, so most probably is the 'witness' of the Spirit referred to in an obscure passage in chapter 5, about which dogmatism would be especially foolish. John is reciting the sure bases of faith: first, gospel history—'He who came by water and blood' (it is almost certain, from the heresy John is opposing, that this means 'by his baptism and his cross'); secondly, the testimony within our own hearts that we do enjoy already an abundant and eternal life; and then 'the water', 'the blood', and 'the Spirit', three witnesses which agree, converging on the same assurance. It is very difficult to be sure what 'water', what 'blood' bear continuing witness within the church, alongside the Spirit, to reassure believers. The Eucharist constantly recalls Christ's shedding of his blood; *John* 6 speaks of our eating Christ's flesh and drinking his blood—evidently in the Lord's Supper; Paul declares that in the Supper we 'proclaim the Lord's death until he comes' (*1 Corinthians* 11:26). Christian baptism provides a visible pattern of Christ's death and resurrection in which believers are 'planted together with him' (*Romans* 6:3–5). In that sense, the sacraments extend through history in concrete form— a dramatic witness in all ages to the fundamental gospel facts. If this is the meaning of the witnessing 'water' and 'blood', then we would expect the witness of the Spirit in the ongoing church to be of the same visible, and objective, kind.

It seems probable, therefore, that John is thinking of the continued manifestation of the Spirit in the church in prophecy, the inspired preaching of the truth borne in upon new hearts; in the victory by which Christians overcome the world; in the young men who have overcome the evil one; in the opposition of Christian hearts to all that is sinful, and their growth in everything that is Christ-like; in the love for God, and for each other, that marks the new life of believers; and in their experience of answered prayer—for these are the features of his readers' lives which John emphasises. If this is his meaning, then the three witnesses within the church are baptism, the Eucharist, and *Christians*, as their lives express the purity, power and enlightenment bestowed by the Spirit. In any case, the general drift of the passage in *1 John* 5 is closely parallel to the understanding of the Spirit in John's gospel: he dwells within the church to testify of the things of Christ, and to convict of sin, and righteousness, and judgement, as the Spirit of truth.

The same is true of the general drift of a second very debateable passage in chapter 2. John there assures the faithful, his 'children' who know the truth and hold to what they heard from the beginning, that they do not need that anyone should teach them, for they possess already an inward instructor, informing their judgement by an inner light. 'You have been anointed by the Holy One, and you all know . . . the anointing which you received from him abides in you, and you have no need that any one should teach you; as his anointing teaches you about everything, and is true, and is no lie, just as it has taught you, abide in him.'

This 'anointing' cannot be some physical act, a laying-on of hands, or anointing with oil, which schismatic leaders could readily imitate; it *instructs* them, and it *abides in* them. It could therefore be the gospel itself as heard from the beginning and which now keeps their judgement right: but an 'anointing' with the *word* is a strange conception. The term looks back to the anointing of Messiah by God's Spirit, foreseen in Isaiah, fulfilled in his baptism, witnessed by the Baptist, testified to in the Nazareth sermon, and recalled by Peter—'how God anointed Jesus of Nazareth with the Holy Spirit and with power' (*Acts* 10:38). As 'anti-Christ' has his followers, for 'many anti-Christs have come' (2:18), so the true 'Christ' (the 'anointed One') has many followers also, who *share his anointing*. The anointing, then, which teaches 'all things' (27, and ? 20) is once more the Spirit of truth promised in the upper room by Jesus to lead disciples into all truth, teach them all things and bring all things to their remembrance. The same

Spirit through whom the gospel had come to the readers, by whom it had been authenticated in their experience, will now lead them through confusion, uncertainty, and division to calm understanding and assured conviction, as they hold fast to that which they first received and rely on the Spirit to lead them into truth, and make plain in time 'all things' that they need to know for daily loyalty.

In all such periods of dissension and bewilderment, perhaps a deeper fear than merely being confused haunts the earnest heart. It is the anxiety lest we be found after all to be far off from Christ; to have lost the blessedness we knew when first we saw the Lord, and failed to go on with Christ to new discoveries and fresh experiences. This will be especially so when the 'new truth' and 'rediscovered emphases' are put forward as 'advanced', 'more spiritual', more truly dedicated or more fully 'blessed' levels of Christian life. The tension of such a time is always between intense desire to be loyal to the past and to 'former days', and the equally intense desire to 'follow on to know the Lord' in every way he has still to reveal himself to us. What if in the end we fall between two opportunities, neither abiding in the Christ we know, nor going forward to make new discoveries of the Spirit?

This would seem to be the need being met by the remaining references to the Spirit in *1 John*:

> By this we know that he abides in us, by the Spirit which he has given us (3:24);
> By this we know that we abide in him and he in us, because he has given us of his own Spirit (4:13).

This offers no evidence *for others* to conclude that all is well between ourselves and God: that requires visible criteria; but for our own hearts, inwardly shaken by the argument around us and the defection of others, the 'interior testimony of the Holy Spirit', an experience venerated through the centuries, is the firmest reassurance we can receive. 'By this we shall know that we are of the truth, and shall assure our hearts before him' (3:19): we *know*, for our own comfort though not for our pride, when the Spirit teaches us further truth about God; when our experience is strangely illumined with meaning *we* could not discover; when we are prompted to attempt new service or accept new responsibility, by the Spirit's leading; when (John says) we find ourselves longing to keep his commandments, to believe, and to love. *We know*, though we can prove to no one else, when we are comforted against adversity, strengthened for unexpected endurance, when our prayer is manifestly heard and answered and 'we receive from him whatever we ask' (5:15); when our peace is inexplicably renewed, our joy sustained, and effectiveness in Christian work is granted to us beyond anything we could contrive or ever deserve. When, in innumerable ways, we are conscious of the Spirit's ministry in and towards ourselves, then we know, whatever others say, that he abides in us and we in him. The more deeply anxious we are to go on with Christ, the more aware we shall be of the dangers of self-deceit, of the need for absolute and self-searching honesty, and of the impossibility of using such inward assurance in any argument or contention. The surer our inward knowledge, the less we shall wish to speak about it: but the inner assurance that the Spirit is still leading and enriching our life, confirming our faith, is even more precious than the promise to guide us in judgement and truth, when the many voices around us are conflicting and our hearts confused.

1 John is peculiarly relevant to our own confused time, when the old divisions that rent the church appear to be dissolving, only to be replaced by new claims and counter-claims, to greater loyalty, or greater 'openness to scripture and the Spirit', to more 'miraculous' or 'charismatic' evidence of God moving in our time—combined, bewilderingly, with new emphasis upon mariolatry, with disregard of inherited patterns of belief and worship, and even occasionally with moral aberrations. In the perplexity of new terms, repeated new translations of the scriptures, new standards and new moral loyalties, new groupings of Christians, sometimes on superficial and emotional grounds constantly threatened by new schisms, the insistence of John that we *can* know the truth, *can* know where we stand, is comforting. If we will walk in the light, love the brethren, hold fast the truth we have proved from the beginning, grow in Christ-likeness, keeping his commandments; if we maintain the confession to which the Spirit led us, and adhere to the fellowship of the truly godly folk who showed us Christ's way; if we observe faithfully the ongoing witness of the Spirit in the one church of Christ, and wait for the inner testimony and illumination within our own souls—then indeed we may reassure our hearts before him, and continue with humble but well-founded confidence to follow the Spirit amid the strife of tongues and the confusion of counsel.

The book of *Revelation*, associated from earliest times

with the gospel and epistle of John, has little to add on the theme of the Spirit, but what it does say falls into the same, mainly 'intellectualist', cast of thought. The Seer of Patmos summons the churches he knows well, in Asia Minor, to heroic resistance against coming persecution, prophesying divine victory at the end, and picturing in marvellous language the glories of heaven, the fierce conflict still to be faced on earth, and the City of God that shall be when God is all in all. Accordingly, John treats of the Spirit as especially the Spirit of prophecy. Repeatedly, the prophetic vision and utterance are explained as the result of 'being in the Spirit' (1:10; 4:2; 17:3; 21:10). When a voice from heaven declares the blessedness of those who die in the Lord, the Spirit confirms: 'Blessed indeed, for they rest from their labours, and their works follow them' (14:13). An ambiguous verse (19:10) identifies the testimony of Jesus with the spirit (? Spirit) of prophecy, as 11:11 could mean not the breath of life but the Spirit of life. The last reference to the Spirit in the Bible shows the Spirit of prophecy, along with the church, awaiting the fulfilment of the divine promises, and crying 'Come!' (22:17).

With similar meaning, the seven letters to the Asian churches each contain the phrase 'He who has an ear, let him hear what the Spirit says to the churches' (2:7, 11, 17, 29; 3:6, 13, 22). Here, too, the Spirit is the source of revelation, but the full implication is still richer: for the word of exhortation and warning from the servant of God speaking in the Spirit (1:1, 10) *is* the word of the risen Christ (1:12, 19; 2:1 etc) and that again *is* what the Spirit says to the churches. The Spirit of revelation is the mouthpiece of the risen Lord, and the mouthpiece of the Spirit within the church is a servant of Christ speaking in the Spirit. The 'seven spirits of God' before the throne (1:4), which Christ 'has' (3:1), which are torches (4:5) and the eyes of the Lamb (5:6) have been identified with the messenger-angels (8:2), with the *six* gifts of the Spirit to Messiah (*Isaiah* 11:2), with the seven lamps and seven eyes of *Zechariah* 4, and with the 'Holy Spirit in his fullness'. Even if the last-named identification could be better defended it would add little to our understanding of the Spirit, except to affirm the Spirit's presence before God's throne, and his joining with God and with Christ in sending grace and peace to the hard-pressed church.

It is remarkable that throughout the 'Johannine' literature—the *Gospel of John*, the *First Epistle of John*, and *Revelation*—the emphasis falls always, not on the Spirit of power and signs, or even on the Spirit who sanctifies, but on the Spirit of truth, and revelation, and reassurance. Intellectually, the Christian may face many problems: confronting the immediate future 'without' Christ; disentangling the confusions of a church beset with error; piercing the more distant future through the fires of persecution and long conflict to see the End God has in store. But whatever the problems for faith, confidence, or endurance, the Johannine writings are unanimous that the answer is the Spirit.

CHAPTER ELEVEN

The question of ministry

It is of the nature of immaturity to resent advice, and for those who offer it to receive no thanks, only criticism. Paul's relations with the church at Corinth were therefore not always happy: the intensity of his concern for them would make him seem interfering and overbearing, while their independence of spirit made him feel rejected by those who owed their very souls to his work. Inevitably, the nature and the grounds of pastoral leadership and ministry would have to be thought out between apostle and people. It is in that connection that the Spirit is discussed in *2 Corinthians*.

Of course familiar truths about the Spirit are also reflected in this epistle. The Spirit is already the possession of all who are Christ's, a distinguishing 'seal' on the people of God, and a guarantee of good things to come (1:22; 5:5). The Spirit witnesses to the world, along with the personal quality and courageous endurance of believers (6:6), though in that list of Christian virtues and activities it is possible that Paul means a (human) 'holiness of spirit'. But one familiar truth finds expression in *2 Corinthians* in one of Christianity's best-known sentences, the 'grace', or Benediction, with which uncountable Christian gatherings and worship-services have concluded, and with which Christians have taken farewell one of another: 'The grace of the Lord Jesus Christ and the love of God and the fellowship of the Holy Spirit be with you all' (13:14).

It is probably through the Benediction that the very name 'the Holy Spirit' is first imprinted on young Christian minds. It is well it should be so, for at once two things are made clear. The Spirit is here at once linked with the Father and with the Son in the unity of the Godhead. The notion of a mere influence or 'magic power' working wonders, an invisible force like electricity, should never linger in minds that *listen* to the Benediction. Moreover, the characteristic work of the Holy Spirit in creating fellowship, which is assumed in *Acts*, *1 Corinthians* and *Ephesians*, is in the Benediction turned to prayer. It is a pity that most who hear, or use, the words assume the meaning to be 'fellowship *with* the Holy Spirit': that is part of the meaning. Paul takes it for granted that all Christians already 'participate' in the Holy Spirit; what he now prayerfully wishes for his readers is something which will be imparted to them, and remain with them, corporately—'be with you all'. This is (as in *Acts*, *Ephesians*) the community-spirit, the fellowship which the Holy Spirit creates among believers as the Spirit of unity. This mutual concern, affection, unity, generosity, fostered by the Spirit among Christians, the Benediction singles out as the 'parting' wish of one Christian to another—along with the grace of Christ and the love of God—to uphold, inspire and comfort while they are absent one from another.

It is however in the special area of Christian ministry that *2 Corinthians* makes its own contribution to

Christian thought about the Spirit. After charges and counter-charges (chapters 1, 10–13) and very sharp tensions (chapter 2), chapter 7 expresses the relief Paul felt upon the arrival of his emissary, Titus, from Corinth with news of a more tractable spirit in the church. The whole of chapters 1 to 9 breathes reconciliation and joy at restored confidence after great strain. Nevertheless, underlying questions could not be ignored. The nature of apostolic ministry, the ground of leadership and authority, must be defined, though with great openness and courtesy. This is the question of ministry: by what right or authority do one or two exercise oversight within a fellowship of believers all of whom are 'priests unto God', all of whom can claim 'all things are lawful to me', all of whom are *one* in Christ Jesus? How is it that leadership, teaching, preaching, evangelism, the conduct of others' worship, pastoral care, and all kinds of service of the gospel and of the church, emerge as functions of 'ministry' in church life: in cruder terms, such as *were* used at Corinth, 'Who does he think he is?'

The fourth chapter of *2 Corinthians* is one of the most self-revealing in all Paul's writing, defining his method, 'commending the truth to every man's conscience in the sight of God'; his message, 'Christ Jesus as Lord'; and his great confidence, 'we faint not . . .' In chapter 5 he explains the motives of his ministry: 'knowing the fear of the Lord . . . the love of Christ constrains us . . .', and also how he sees the whole position of the Christian ministry as an *ambassadorship* for God, a commission to call men to be reconciled to God through the death of Christ for our sin. Chapter 6 rehearses the many ways in which by personal example and endurance the messenger must commend the message in the sight of all men. But the foundation of this whole discussion is laid in chapter 3, in the new covenant 'in the Spirit' and the 'dispensation of the Spirit'.

The argument is very condensed, but important. It begins with a simple reference to inter-church letters of recommendation, of which rival claimants to authority at Corinth apparently made much. Paul scorns the need of these: the Corinthian Christians themselves are the best testimonials to his ministry, *living* letters, written by the Spirit himself, to be known and read by all the city. But Paul denies any sense of self-sufficiency for the great work he undertakes. It is not his gifts or abilities that make him a minister, but God, 'who has qualified us to be ministers of a new covenant'.

That phrase sets Paul off at a tangent. He appears to leave the subject of ministry in order to compare old and new regimes in the service of God. As a Pharisee and a teacher of Judaism, Paul had been a minister of the old covenant: he is now a 'qualified' minister of the new covenant; the difference holds his attention through a dozen verses. He has not however actually deserted his theme, or the real questions raised at Corinth, for he then proceeds at once with 'having this ministry . . . we do not lose heart.' What has caught his imagination is the contrast between his present ministry as a Christian apostle and his former ministry of the Jewish law, and he elaborates that contrast in fascinating, and very relevant, detail.

The old covenant-relationship with God was expressed in a written code 'carved in letters on stone',

136

an external regulation of human behaviour by commandments enforced by sanctions; the new covenant found expression 'in the Spirit', by a living inspiration binding the hearts of men in loyalty and love toward God, as Jeremiah promised the new covenant would do, with its 'law written upon the heart'. The old covenant, in consequence, though ordained for life resulted in death: 'the written code kills . . . a dispensation of death'. As Paul explains elsewhere, 'I was alive once apart from the law, but when the commandment came, sin revived and I died; the very commandment which promised life proved to be death to me . . .' (*Romans* 7:9, 10). The new covenant results in life: 'the dispensation of the Spirit' is contrasted with the dispensation of death': 'the Spirit gives life'.

The old covenant, through man's inability to keep its terms, turned out to be a 'dispensation of condemnation'; the new covenant proved to be a 'dispensation of righteousness', for what the law could not do in man, God accomplished by the rule of the Spirit of life in Christ Jesus, fulfilling the righteousness of the law in us (*Romans* 8:2–4). Nevertheless, despite death and condemnation, even the old covenant possessed splendour, such that the Israelites could not look at Moses' face because of its brightness, reflecting God's glory. But the new covenant possesses infinitely greater splendour, so great as to outshine the splendour of the old, and so permanent as to outlast it; for the glow on Moses' face faded very soon: the glory of the new covenant will never pass away.

Paul takes that further. The old covenant was necessarily one of only partial revelation; Israel could not take the full truth offered to them. Moses himself veiled his face so that they should not see the glory fade; and the veil remains now on the hardened heart of Israel when they hear the old covenant read: they do not even yet comprehend. 'Only through Christ is that veil taken away': 'when a man turns to the Lord the veil is removed'. The new covenant therefore is one of full understanding, of unveiled face, of full and immediate access to the glory of the Lord. And so, whereas the old covenant was one of law, tending to bondage, the new covenant of the Spirit is one of freedom: 'where the Spirit of the Lord is, there is freedom'. And in such free acceptance into the presence of the Lord by the Spirit, we too reflect in ourselves, even as Moses did, the unfading glory of the Lord whom we behold, being changed step by step into the same image by the Lord who is the Spirit.

If, admitting the fascination of this contrast, we question its relevance to ourselves, that is precisely because the Spirit has for us completely replaced the law, the new covenant superseded the old, so that we no longer even feel the strong obligation to the past which Paul felt and wrestled with. For all Jews this was a serious problem. The novelty of the Christian faith seemed disloyalty to the ancient revelation. In *John* 2 the old temple is replaced by the body of Christ as the centre of worship—a blow to Jewish hearts. In *Philippians* 3, Paul insists on the validity of the new regime: we are the true circumcision, who worship God in spirit, glory in Christ Jesus, and put no confidence in the flesh. In *Romans* 4, the faith by which Christians are saved is shown to be consistent with the faith of Abraham and David. Here in *2 Corinthians*, the nagging question comes nearer home, as Paul compares his present ministry with that he exercised under the old regime. To be minister under the old covenant had been the highest honour earth afforded; in it lay a divine commission, with spiritual authority and a life purpose. As a minister, now, of the new covenant—and of churches like that at Corinth!—what replaced the spiritual status, the high honour, that he had lost? It was vital to Paul that he should understand the direct relation of his present position to the past and to his former faith; and to feel that as minister of the new covenant, he held a position in fact more exalted, and privileged, and inspiring, than anything he had known.

So point by point he assures his own heart that the new covenant excels the old, a covenant of inspiration, not compulsion; of life, not death; of righteousness, not condemnation; of surpassing and unfading splendour; a covenant of completed revelation and open understanding, and so of freedom; and one that reflects upon ourselves the glory of the Lord. And he is a minister of that new covenant! It is noteworthy that Paul does not here defend his ministry by recounting the call of God and the divine providence that made him an apostle (as he does in *Galatians* 1); nor by rehearsing his labours, visions, and sufferings (as he does in *2 Corinthians* 10–13). Instead, he dwells on the inherent privileges of the Christian ministry itself. This is probably because he is not meeting others' challenges to his personal position, but the independent Corinthians' criticisms of pastoral leadership in general: the questioning, not merely why Paul thinks he is a minister, but why any 'gifted' church should want ministry at all. The basis of Paul's reply is that the new covenant is 'of the Spirit', who requires his human channels. 'Not that we are sufficient of ourselves to claim anything as coming from us; our sufficiency is from God, who has qualified us to be ministers of a new covenant . . . in the Spirit.'

In so arguing, Paul has added yet again to the New Testament understanding of the Spirit, as source, inspiration, validation, and splendour, of the Christian ministry. He means at least three things and first, that *the Christian ministry is a ministry, or 'dispensation' of the Spirit*. That could mean simply a 'service' of the Spirit (so the Greek, literally); but it could also mean that the ministry 'ministers the Spirit to man', 'dispenses the Spirit', in the same way that the law 'dispensed death' (*NEB*), and Paul and his colleagues 'dispensed' the new covenant (*NEB*), and God's ambassadors conferred, or brought about, the reconciliation Christ had wrought upon the cross (so 5:18 in a parallel Greek phrase). If precise translation of an ambiguous word is debatable, there remains no doubt that Paul regarded the crucial aim and outcome of his work as bringing others into the life and experience of the Spirit. In such terms he recalled his first coming to Corinth (*1 Corinthians* 2:4), as a 'demonstration of the Spirit and of power'; he spoke so of his arrival in Galatia (*Galatians* 3:2–5), and in Thessalonica (*1 Thessalonians* 1:6).

The teacher is delighted with evidence of imparted ideas, kindled minds; the pastor is encouraged by evidence of strengthened and wiser Christian lives. But the evangelist looks for evidence of imparted *life*, for a bestowal, a sharing, of the *Spirit*. Indeed, Paul somewhat tartly reminds the Corinthians that they may have countless guides in Christ, but they do not have many fathers: 'For I became your father in Christ Jesus through the gospel' (*1 Corinthians* 4:15).

Others. like the Pharisees, may impose or interpret laws, disseminate information, instruct in doctrine; others, like the priests, may perform rituals; others may counsel and edify: but the heart of the Christian ministry lies in leading new souls into the experience of the Spirit, and in mediating by the gospel the bestowal of life itself, 'a dispensing of the Spirit'.

Secondly, and for that reason, *the Christian ministry rests upon the direct inspiration of Christian hearts by the Spirit*, whose inward rule becomes the new law of the Christian's conduct. The most that the minister can do is 'by the open statement of the truth . . . to commend to every man's conscience in the sight of God' the things given him to speak (4:2): the rest is the work of the Spirit within the soul, leading men to understanding, to light, and on to faith (compare 4:6). 'Not that we are sufficient of ourselves to claim anything as coming from us' (3:5); the only 'Paraclete' is the Spirit: the pastor's counsel, encouragement, teaching, warning—his *paraclesis*—is but the open way for that divine ministry of the Spirit within another soul. An overbearing, dictatorial ministry, which strives to do by force of personality, or by institutional authority, or by threat and blackmail, what only the Spirit can accomplish, working from within, has no place in the New Testament. A ministry of the Spirit does not seek to indoctrinate men with the gospel, but to lead them to make their own discoveries of truth; it does not seek to impose its own pattern of conduct upon others, but to lead them into that surrender to the Spirit in which is freedom. Such a ministry may call for unusual self-effacement and humility in those called nevertheless to lead: its reward lies in the mature, and truly spiritual, independence of converts who learn to stand or fall to their own Master.

Thirdly, *the fruit of such a Christian ministry is in living witnesses to the gospel*, whose whole manner and bearing, conduct and speech and joy, recommend the gospel to their neighbours. Especially do such 'fruits of ministry' exhibit the qualities of people of the new covenant: as having true life, righteousness, liberty, understanding, and the taste of splendour. Paul's figure suggests that such a church is set down amidst the disreputable city of Corinth as a mail-box full of 'open letters', addressed by Christ to the passing citizens: each letter is an individual Christian, whose personal story has been written by the Spirit on a single human heart. Such living testimonies not only spread the gospel, they validate the ministry that produces and sustains them. By such living 'letters of recommendation' the gospel is written afresh in each generation, and the original inspiration is perpetuated in a way which no other 'scripture', however sacred or indispensable, can attain. Doubtless this was very obviously true of those first generations when the church possessed no Christian scripture of her own; but it remains true for every successive generation, that the Christian Bible for the outside world is the living Christian.

By so rewriting the Christian testimony in faithful hearts, the Spirit 'unveils' Christ again in each successive generation. Paul makes great homiletic play with the story of Moses' veil. At first the brightness of Moses' face necessitated some filtering shade; but a second reason for the veil was to hide the fading of that splendour, whereas the glory of the new regime is both brighter and more permanent. The veil then shifts to the minds of those who hear Moses read, obscuring from hardened hearts the truth they ought to comprehend: but that veil is done away in Christ. Somewhere in all this it is being suggested that the minister's supreme task is in both senses to lift the veil that hides the Christ: from Christ himself, by proclaiming his beauty that men should desire him and his glory that men should trust him; and from the unbelieving heart, by winsome persuasion kindling faith. Nor will the true minister be much troubled at Paul's assumption that such a ministry will be shared by every 'walking epistle' read by men: so much the better if all the church 'preach not ourselves but Jesus Christ as Lord' (4:5). Nevertheless, the writing of each human testimony, and the unveiling of the Christ, remain always the work of the Spirit.

And it will consist in more than words, and isolated Christian deeds. The letters mysteriously become mirrors, and the testimony about Christ is illustrated by radiant reflections. Minister and people ('we all . . .') in the end unveil Christ most effectively by reproducing his glory in Christlike lives. Admitted together into the divine presence, as Moses was, they catch the reflection of him whom they behold, and come forth unveiled to let the world see his radiance. By such experience of worship, repeated and increasing ('from glory to glory . . .') they grow into his likeness, until their own lives beam eternal glory into the dark places of the earth. This too, says Paul, the whole transfiguring operation, comes from the Lord who is the Spirit.

We are told so often that the Christian ministry in these days is a vocation that has lost its identity, a dedicated profession in search of a role in modern society, an elite coterie hunting for a *raison d'etre* commensurate with its former dignity. Guidelines for that search include a better understanding of the immense demand for truly pastoral service created by the tensions, disappointments, confusion, and vacancy of modern life: but not all ministers are satisfied to become agents of a religious sociology alongside the secular rehabilitation machinery. Nor do the usual historical and ecclesiastical 'justifications' for Christian priesthood satisfy hearts hard-pressed by frustration and undermined with doubt. Paul's treatment of the question of ministry in *2 Corinthians* suggests a different approach again: let the minister learn to see himself *less* as the appointed agent of the church, spokesman of a tradition, or enabler of the inadequate, and *more* as the vehicle of the divine Spirit, dispensing life.

The central biblical concept of man sees him as the focus and battle-ground of forces, energies, and purposes greater than his own, either for evil or for good as he shall choose. To be a vehicle, that is man's glory, or his doom. So the highest significance that any man's life can achieve is to become the channel of the redeeming power of God, the living vehicle of the living Spirit who strives with men for their salvation. This is the conception of ministry that underlies *2 Corinthians* 3; it could scarcely find more dramatic, or more realistic illustration than in *2 Corinthians* 12. Beset with 'weakness', harassed by 'a thorn . . . in the flesh', evidently something painful and disabling, aware alike of satanic hindering and of unanswered prayers, and facing all the time from outsiders insults, hardship, persecution and calamities, Paul sounds at his lowest ebb of confidence. The notion that he is after all but the channel of invasive energies enables him to regain insight and courage. He realises that divine power is most perfectly in evidence when the instrument, the vehicle, is at its weakest, neither obstructing the flow of grace to others by getting in the way, nor drawing attention to its own prowess and efficiency. So with utter realism Paul declares that he would the more gladly boast of his weaknesses, *so that* the power of Christ may the more clearly rest upon him. 'For when I am weak, then I am strong.'

This, at least, would be Paul's briefing in the Christian worker's search for 'social identity': if the question be what is the rationale of ministry in a secular world, Paul's answer is—the Spirit.

CHAPTER TWELVE

'No one can . . . except by the Holy Spirit'

To summarise a book as rich, as varied, as vigorously alive and developing, as the New Testament is an impossible task; hardly less so if one concentrates on a single theme. Even to draw threads together incurs the danger of entangling them, and distorting the balance of truth. Both the difficulty, and the danger, seem especially acute when the subject is the Spirit.

This is partly, no doubt, because the topic is contentious; but partly too because what the New Testament says about the Spirit is so many-sided, and inexhaustible. We have seen the Holy Spirit successively as: the Spirit of communication, endowing the early church with boldness, prophetic authority, and 'tongues' (*Acts, 1 Corinthians*), and with courage and wisdom to defend the faith in days of persecution, and to convict the world (*Matthew, John*); as the Spirit of power authenticating the gospel and equipping the various types of ministry within the church (*Acts, Thessalonians, 1 Corinthians*); as the Spirit of holiness and *paraclesis* sanctifying individual character and corporate church life (*Acts, 1 Corinthians*), and making salvation work by the power of God within the soul (*Romans*); as the Spirit who promotes and safeguards personal freedom (*2 Corinthians, Galatians*); as the Spirit superintending the life of the church and guiding individuals (*Acts, 1 Corinthians*); as the Spirit of fellowship, unity, love, who unites diverse elements in one living body of Christ (*Acts, 1 Corinthians, Ephesians*); and—constantly emphasised though often neglected today—as the Spirit of truth, exercising an 'intellectual' ministry of reminding, teaching, leading forward, convicting, fortifying, bestowing wisdom, clearing confusion and reassuring faith (*John, 1 John, 1 Corinthians*). In all these ways we have seen the Spirit empowering and working through every Christian worker ministering in the church of Christ (*2 Corinthians*).

Plainly, the 'charismatic experience' offered to Christians by the New Testament is wide as human need, varied as the human temperament, manifold as human experience, and always a positive enrichment of personality in just those areas in which an individual Christian life happens most to require completion.

Such richness of truth defies neat summarising; but three things can be underlined, to which the whole New Testament bears witness. Inheriting a partly impersonal idea of the Spirit of God as the invisible power that comes upon chosen individuals, the New Testament universalises, moralises, and personalises man's thought of the Spirit, irrevocably. It is *universalised* because what had been reserved for outstanding and rare figures in the Old Testament becomes in the New the common possession of the people of God. As Joel had promised to old and young, to male and female, to masters, servants, handmaids, and as the gospels and epistles constantly take for granted, *all Christians are made partakers of the Spirit: not to possess the Spirit is not to be Christ's.*

The idea of the Spirit is *moralised*, in that sometimes

in the Old Testament no relation appears between the personal character of the bearers of the Spirit (Samson, Balaam) and their great privilege; nor is their use of the Spirit's power always admirable: whereas in the New Testament, the Spirit is above all the *Holy* Spirit, the source of renewed character and the one who reproduces in us the likeness of Christ. The characteristic of New Testament teaching on the Spirit is precisely that it sees him less and less as the bestower of spectacular 'gifts', the generator of the inexplicable 'power', and more and more as the spring of divine life, the source and creator of Christian morality, of whose presence in the soul every Christian virtue is the natural 'fruit'.

Especially is the idea of the Spirit once for all *personalised* in the New Testament, by the constant and close association (hardly falling short of identification) of the Spirit with Christ. He is ever Christ's 'other self', as John represents him: 'the form of the contemporary Christ in the experience of believers', 'the Lord the Spirit'. In *Luke* no less than in *John*, in *Acts*, throughout the epistles, and in *Revelation*, the unity of the Spirit with Christ is simply assumed; the ministry of the Spirit is at once the Spirit's own initiative, and yet ascribed almost indiscriminately to the Spirit and to the risen Christ. Sub-personal terms for the Spirit sometimes linger in the New Testament, but they never obscure the personality of the Spirit.

Much misunderstanding would be avoided, not to say repugnance, and even fear, if this *maturing* of the Christian understanding of the Holy Spirit were always kept in mind. 'The Spirit' is 'the Spirit of Jesus' (*Acts* 16:7): his purpose is to enrich, endow, equip, sanctify, and teach: he seeks to be to each

Christian soul all that Christ was to the Eleven. It is a thousand pities that in many Christian minds the whole idea of a Spirit-filled life is associated only with the eccentric, the emotional, the inexplicable, with egocentric displays of useless capacities, with fanatical dogmatism and the cult of 'spiritual magic', with second sight, and even with the occult. It is essential that earnest Christians shall not be repelled by the emphasis on bizarre 'manifestations' from openness to all that the Spirit could do in their lives. The 'back to Corinth' movement has done much to remind the whole church of the promise of the Spirit: it has done much also, unfortunately, to insulate many against any true understanding and experience of the manifold ministry which the Spirit offers to them.

It is no less essential that earnest Christians shall not be misled by the selection of particular 'gifts and manifestations' of the Spirit as typical pattern-experiences, to be sought or emulated by other Christians. A truly astonishing variety of expressions and metaphors is used in the New Testament to describe the almost innumerable ways in which the Spirit will make his presence and power known to the Christian, apportioning 'to each one individually as he will' (*1 Corinthians* 12:11). To 'have' or 'possess' the Spirit, even 'the supply of the Spirit', 'God gave them the Spirit', and 'to partake' of the Spirit, are used by Paul or by Peter, in the sense of having the aid and ministry of the Spirit, though never with any implication that the Spirit himself becomes ours to direct or use as *we* will. The 'descent' of the Spirit, his 'resting' on Jesus, his 'falling upon' Cornelius, his being 'poured forth' upon us, our 'receiving' the Spirit, and the Spirit 'inbreathing', are all phrases that emphasise the *invasive* presence of the Spirit in our personality, coming (so to speak) from without, from above, into our lives, as we are open to welcome him.

That such incoming of the Spirit creates a totally new self and a new life-situation, is implied in 'born . . . of the Spirit'; expressions like 'baptised in/with the Spirit', being 'in the Spirit', we saw to be parallel to being 'in Christ', as the Spirit becomes the very atmosphere and setting of our daily life. On the other hand, 'indwelt by the Spirit', the Christian and the church being 'shrines of the Spirit', puts the same truth, the intimate and constant relation of the Spirit and ourselves, the other way: he is in us as we are in him.

The high hours when this experience reaches its zenith in zeal, joy, effectiveness, and unhindered outflow, are spoken of as times of the 'filling' of the Spirit, as though all else were crowded out. Then our personal weakness and inadequacy are overwhelmed and we are 'clothed' with the Spirit's power; our reluctance and wilfulness are overruled as we are 'bound in the Spirit'. The inner reassurance so gained is the 'witness' of the Spirit to our spirit that we are sons of God, the Spirit 'teaching all things . . . bringing all things to our remembrance'. In all these ways—and the list cannot be made exhaustive— Christians are privileged to share in the messianic 'anointing' of the Christ, and are sealed as his own until the day of redemption. To stereotype so infinitely varied a privilege, in order to promote a cult of this special gift or that peculiar manifestation, is to limit and distort the manifold ministry of the Spirit.

But not only is it unscriptural to isolate particular

ministries of the Spirit and exalt them as alone 'valid', and to be sought after: the New Testament is curiously reticent about what Christians should do, or may do, to experience more often, or more fully, the Spirit's infilling. As we have seen, teaching about the Spirit is distributed through the New Testament with marked inequality: nowhere is the experience and manifestation of the Spirit the direct or central theme, as something requiring to be urged upon the readers. That Christians are born of the Spirit, already 'possess' the Spirit, and are 'partakers' of the Spirit being everywhere assumed, no prayer for his coming, or directions how to seek or receive him, certainly not how to 'deserve' him, are ever found. The promise of the Spirit is 'to you and to your children and to all that are afar off, every one whom the Lord our God calls to him' (*Acts* 2:39).

Indeed, throughout the New Testament there are only five imperatives or commands related to the experience of the Spirit. These are: not to 'quench the Spirit', evidently (as we saw) an instruction not to forbid self-expression to the Spirit-gifted in the worship assemblies. 'Do not grieve the Spirit', as the context shows, means do not by sinful and anti-social behaviour hinder the sense of the Spirit's presence in the Christian community. The command to 'walk by the Spirit', with its Old Testament background and its contrast with obedience to the law, evidently means 'live daily by the Spirit's direction'. Jude urges that we 'pray in the Spirit', and so does Paul. And Paul adds, 'Be filled with the Spirit' in direct contrast with being filled with wine, which suggests that we should at all times be receptive, responsive, open to a fuller experience of the Spirit's ministry towards us and through us (*1 Thessalonians* 5:19; *Ephesians* 4:30; *Galatians* 5:16, 25; *Jude* 20; *Ephesians* 6:18; 5:18).

It is surely remarkable, and very significant, that except for these few, and natural, exhortations, *all the many New Testament references to the Spirit are statements* of what he does, or will do, or is given to do, in Christian life. In this realm, as in the gospel as a whole, we are receptive, not entirely passive, perhaps, but in no sense manipulating the situation, taking the initiative, or controlling the Spirit, but always receiving, responding, being ministered to, by the Spirit who comes in Christ's name to fulfil his promises to his own.

The one emphasis of the New Testament which touches immediately upon the inadequacy of our experience in these days of what the Spirit could do, is that around which our study has been centred: the Spirit is ever introduced and presented as the answer to our practical problems and necessities. The Holy Spirit is no fancy doctrine for fanatics to organise field-days about: but the solution of specific needs and difficulties in living the Christian life and facing the outside world.

'No one can . . . except by the Holy Spirit.' The words of Paul to Corinth (*1 Corinthians* 12:3) relate specifically to calling Jesus Lord, the hallmark so to speak of a truly Christian inspiration. It would appear to be an over-statement: such a confession requires only a little breath and a little boldness! But Paul is thinking of the crucial public confession of Christ, first required by Jesus himself at Caesarea Philippi, which each New Testament believer echoed in baptism; in that context, calling Jesus 'Lord' commits the speaker to reorientation of life under the lordship of Christ. This could not happen, Paul implies, but for the convicting and converting power of the Holy Spirit, bringing the soul to such decision, and to accept the changes and the risks involved, strengthening the convert for the new life begun in Christ. As Jesus said, '. . . unless one is born of water and the Spirit, he cannot enter the kingdom of God' (*John* 3:5). But if even this elementary step in Christian experience is impossible without the Spirit, how much more true that is of every succeeding step! 'No one can . . .' do *anything* Christian '. . . except by the Holy Spirit.'

This has been the conviction behind the practical approach to the New Testament's teaching on the Spirit, because it is the New Testament's own approach. To the problems involved in communication, in presenting Christ, in evangelising the world; to the problems of living as Christians without the Master's physical presence; to the problem how salvation by faith alone really operates; to problems of emotional immaturity in individuals and in the church; to the special Christian problem of reconciling freedom with discipline; to the difficulty of discerning the truth amid confusing claims; to the special church problems of diversity and divisiveness, and the emergence of leadership among equals—to one and all, the New Testament says, the solution lies in the experience of the Spirit: and this is the only way in which the Spirit is set forward in the apostolic writings. He does not speak of himself: he takes of the things of Christ and applies them to our needs and difficulties. He is the divine enabler—one is tempted to say, the divine trouble-shooter; the one who 'comes alongside to help' when the way is rough, the task immense, the difficulties multiply, and faith is small. Not *only* then: for without him we would not be Christians at all; but to make us Christians, to keep us Christians, and to use us as Christians, is his ministry, always nearest when the need is greatest.

Does it not follow from this presentation of the truth that our experience of the Spirit will be commensurate with the size of the problems we tackle? That our experience of the Spirit's power and leading, of the equipment and enjoyment he can bestow, will always be just as wide, as deep, as far-reaching, as the tasks we attempt and the difficulties we face up to—no less, *and no more.* Christians who sit and wait for power will be given the power—to sit and wait. If the divine equipment and enabling are ever given to be *used*, then the use made determines the power received. Huddling around our fifteen-watt lamps we complain of the poor current! We sit over silent and ineffective ecclesiastical machinery unaware that the fuse is at our end!

The supreme example of this principle in later Christian centuries is seen in one man who in talk and temperament would be counted least 'charismatic', in the modern sense, of all Christian leaders: yet under God he transformed the total scene for the Christian church, not only of the west but throughout the world. Cobbler, schoolteacher, lay-preacher, village pastor, botanist, scholar, linguist (helping translation in thirty languages!), founder of the first Christian University in the east, William Carey pioneered the first-ever church-based missionary movement, that immediately bloomed into fourteen British—beside

154

European and American—societies. All that has followed: the world church spread throughout the globe; medical and educational missions following the gospel into the third world; immeasurable missionary exploration and development; Bible translation and distribution in every land; the international ecumenical movement; the flood of Christian generosity and of dedicated Christian people devoted to the work of Christ under all possible conditions, in every variety of peril, often accepting martyrdom; the immense enrichment of the western churches in reflex blessing—the whole modern, world-wide, church-based missionary movement of the Spirit can seriously be traced back, in human terms, to one man's persistence. 'Unquestionably the very foremost name of our times in the whole Christian world' was the tribute of John Foster, the contemporary essayist; echoed by John Foster, Professor of Church History, in our century, with the words 'one of the greatest pioneer missionaries and Bible translators the church has ever known'. And if we seek one crucial, watershed moment in that man's life, as the moment of creation of two whole centuries of astonishing advance, it must be a sermon, preached at Nottingham, with two heads: 'Expect great things from God; Attempt great things for God.'

That is illustration only, but it is apt example of the way the Spirit manifests himself: attempt great things, and the expected great things *happen*. If we go forward we find the Spirit there, ahead of us: if we stay at home, we wonder 'where be all the miracles our fathers told us of?' (*Judges* 6:13). If the Spirit is always God's answer to the problem, and we shun the problem, we shall never discover what the Spirit might have done.

Modern Christians on the whole are persuaded that 'never were things so difficult for Christianity!' The less they know of the church's history, the more sure they are that the faith was never in such peril, nor the future so dark. Certainly the church has some tremendous problems to confront, as the intellectual climate hardens into secularist and sensual patterns; as the struggle for political power once again brings out all the violence and ambition that bedevil the world; as the familiar forms of church life break up under the tensions of a new generation's impatient challenge and demand for change; as the weakness of our disunity becomes ever more apparent under increasing pressures from without. Thank God, there are pressures also from within: the deepest problems of all are posed by the hunger for freer and fuller expression of truly spiritual life, breaking out of the conventionally Christian, breaking through the customs that have long history but no vital meaning. Once again in the church of Christ the new wine demands new wineskins. But that is just such a time, and such are just the problems, to which the answer is—the Spirit.

Said John Warr, who led Carey to Christ, 'My heart is all window to him'.

FOR FURTHER STUDY

This introductory, and severely practical, study has deliberately avoided theological implications and the discussion of other views. General readers desiring to check any point, or to pursue the theme, will still find help in two older books: A L Humphries, *The Holy Spirit in Faith and Experience*, and W H Griffith Thomas, *The Holy Spirit of God*. Among innumerable devotional studies are G Campbell Morgan, *The Spirit of God*; J R W Stott, *Baptism and Fullness of the Holy Spirit*; and (small but invaluable) McConkey, *The Threefold Secret of the Holy Spirit*.

Serious students might well begin with the always lucid and satisfying James Denney (Hastings' *Dictionary of Christ and the Gospels*, vol i, page 731—'The Holy Spirit'), and move on to G W H Lampe, *Seal of the Spirit*; C K Barrett, *Holy Spirit in Gospel Tradition*; H Wheeler Robinson, *Christian Experience of the Holy Spirit* (for the wider implications); by the time they reach J G D Dunn, *Baptism and the Holy Spirit*, and J V Taylor, *The Go-Between God*, they will have entered upon a vast literature that exceeds any man's time or capacity to digest, if investigation is ever to give place to experience. For the so-called 'charismatic' approach, the best beginning is probably T A Smail, *Reflected Glory*.

Other recent additions to a growing literature are: G S Hendry: *The Holy Spirit in Christian Theology* (SCM Press)—'a short clear statement along traditional lines'; H Berkhof: *The Doctrine of the Holy Spirit* (Epworth Press)—'a short and first-rate introduction';

Michael Green: *I Believe in the Holy Spirit* (Hodder and Stoughton); and Michael Harper (editor): *Bishops' Move* (by six Anglican bishops; Hodder and Stoughton). From the wider viewpoint of a Roman Catholic missionary: D Dorrs: *Remove the Heart of Stone* (Gill and Macmillan).

Index to Scripture References

160

162